# WILEY Practice*Planners*

Arthur E. Jongsma, Jr., Series Editor

# *Helping therapists help their clients*

**Treatment Planners** cover all the necessary elements for developing formal treatment plans, including detailed problem definitions, long-term goals, short-term objectives, therapeutic interventions, and DSM™ diagnoses.

- ❏ The Complete Adult Psychotherapy Treatment Planner, Fifth Edition* .......... 978-1-118-06786-4 / $60.00
- ❏ The Child Psychotherapy Treatment Planner, Fifth Edition* ......................... 978-1-118-06785-7 / $60.00
- ❏ The Adolescent Psychotherapy Treatment Planner, Fifth Edition* ................ 978-1-118-06784-0 / $60.00
- ❏ The Addiction Treatment Planner, Fifth Edition* ........................................... 978-1-118-41475-0 / $60.00
- ❏ The Couples Psychotherapy Treatment Planner, Second Edition* ................ 978-1-119-06312-4 / $60.00
- ❏ The Group Therapy Treatment Planner, Second Edition* .............................. 978-1-119-07318-5 / $60.00
- ❏ The Family Therapy Treatment Planner, Second Edition* ............................. 978-1-119-06307-0 / $60.00
- ❏ The Older Adult Psychotherapy Treatment Planner, Second Edition* ........... 978-1-119-06311-7 / $60.00
- ❏ The Employee Assistance (EAP) Treatment Planner ..................................... 978-0-471-24709-8 / $60.00
- ❏ The Gay and Lesbian Psychotherapy Treatment Planner............................... 978-0-471-35080-4 / $60.00
- ❏ The Crisis Counseling and Traumatic Events Treatment Planner,
  Second Edition*............................................................................................. 978-1-119-06315-5 / $60.00
- ❏ The Social Work and Human Services Treatment Planner* .......................... 978-1-119-07323-9 / $60.00
- ❏ The Continuum of Care Treatment Planner................................................... 978-0-471-19568-9 / $60.00
- ❏ The Behavioral Medicine Treatment Planner ................................................ 978-0-471-31923-8 / $60.00
- ❏ The Intellectual and Developmental Disability Treatment Planner* ............. 978-1-119-07330-7 / $60.00
- ❏ The Special Education Treatment Planner..................................................... 978-0-471-38872-2 / $60.00
- ❏ The Severe and Persistent Mental Illness Treatment Planner,
  Second Edition*............................................................................................. 978-1-119-06309-6 / $60.00
- ❏ The Personality Disorders Treatment Planner, Second Edition* ................... 978-0-470-90868-6 / $60.00
- ❏ The Rehabilitation Psychology Treatment Planner ....................................... 978-0-471-35178-8 / $60.00
- ❏ The Pastoral Counseling Treatment Planner.................................................. 978-0-471-25416-4 / $60.00
- ❏ The Juvenile Justice and Residential Care Treatment Planner* .................... 978-1-119-07328-4 / $60.00
- ❏ The School Counseling and School Social Work Treatment Planner,
  Second Edition*............................................................................................. 978-1-119-06309-4 / $60.00
- ❏ The Psychopharmacology Treatment Planner ............................................... 978-0-471-43322-4 / $60.00
- ❏ The Probation and Parole Treatment Planner*.............................................. 978-1-119-07328-4 / $60.00
- ❏ The Suicide and Homicide Risk Assessment & Prevention
  Treatment Planner*....................................................................................... 978-1-119-07331-4 / $60.00
- ❏ The Speech-Language Pathology Treatment Planner.................................... 978-0-471-27504-6 / $60.00
- ❏ The College Student Counseling Treatment Planner .................................... 978-0-471-46708-3 / $60.00
- ❏ The Parenting Skills Treatment Planner* ...................................................... 978-1-119-07312-3 / $60.00
- ❏ The Early Childhood Education Intervention Treatment Planner ................. 978-0-471-65962-4 / $60.00
- ❏ The Co-Occurring Disorders Treatment Planner*.......................................... 978-1-119-07319-2 / $60.00
- ❏ The Sexual Abuse Victim and Sexual Offender Treatment Planner* ............ 978-1-119-07332-1 / $60.00
- ❏ The Complete Women's Psychotherapy Treatment Planner ......................... 978-0-470-03983-0 / $60.00
- ❏ The Veterans and Active Duty Military Psychotherapy
  Treatment Planner*....................................................................................... 978-1-119-06308-7 / $60.00

*Updated to DSM-5™

The **Complete Treatment and Homework Planners** series of books combines our bestselling *Treatment Planners* and *Homework Planners* into one easy-to-use, all-in-one resource for mental health professionals treating clients suffering from the most commonly diagnosed disorders.

- ❏ The Complete Depression Treatment and Homework Planner .................... 978-0-471-64515-3 / $60.00
- ❏ The Complete Anxiety Treatment and Homework Planner .......................... 978-0-471-64548-1 / $60.00

**Over 1,000,000 Practice*Planners*® sold**

**WILEY**

# WILEY Practice*Planners*

**Homework Planners** feature dozens of behaviorally based, ready-to-use assignments that are designed for use between sessions, as well as a website containing all of the assignments—allowing you to customize them to suit your unique client needs.

- ❏ Couples Therapy Homework Planner, Second Edition ................................. 978-0-470-52266-0 / $60.00
- ❏ Child Psychotherapy Homework Planner, Fifth Edition ............................... 978-1-118-07674-3 / $60.00
- ❏ Child Therapy Activity and Homework Planner ........................................... 978-0-471-25684-7 / $60.00
- ❏ Adolescent Psychotherapy Homework Planner, Fifth Edition ...................... 978-1-118-07673-6 / $60.00
- ❏ Addiction Treatment Homework Planner, Fifth Edition ............................... 978-1-118-56059-4 / $60.00
- ❏ Family Therapy Homework Planner, Second Edition ................................... 978-0-470-50439-0 / $60.00
- ❏ Grief Counseling Homework Planner ........................................................... 978-0-471-43318-7 / $60.00
- ❏ Group Therapy Homework Planner ............................................................. 978-0-471-41822-1 / $60.00
- ❏ School Counseling and School Social Work Homework Planner,
  Second Edition ............................................................................................ 978-1-118-41038-7 / $60.00
- ❏ Adult Psychotherapy Homework Planner, Fifth Edition ............................... 978-1-118-07672-9 / $60.00
- ❏ Parenting Skills Homework Planner ............................................................ 978-0-471-48182-9 / $60.00
- ❏ Veterans and Active Duty Military Psychotherapy Homework Planner ...... 978-0-470-89052-3 / $60.00

**Progress Notes Planners** contain complete prewritten progress notes for each presenting problem in the companion Treatment Planners.

- ❏ The Adult Psychotherapy Progress Notes Planner ...................................... 978-1-118-06675-1 / $60.00
- ❏ The Adolescent Psychotherapy Progress Notes Planner ............................. 978-1-118-06676-8 / $60.00
- ❏ The Severe and Persistent Mental Illness Progress Notes Planner ............ 978-0-470-18014-3 / $60.00
- ❏ The Child Psychotherapy Progress Notes Planner ...................................... 978-1-118-06677-5 / $60.00
- ❏ The Addiction Progress Notes Planner ........................................................ 978-1-118-54296-5 / $60.00
- ❏ The Couples Psychotherapy Progress Notes Planner .................................. 978-0-470-93691-7 / $60.00
- ❏ The Family Therapy Progress Notes Planner .............................................. 978-0-470-44884-7 / $60.00
- ❏ The Veterans and Active Duty Military Psychotherapy
  Progress Notes Planner ............................................................................... 978-0-470-44097-1 / $60.00

**Client Education Handout Planners** contain elegantly designed handouts that can be printed out from online and provide information on a wide range of psychological and emotional disorders and life skills issues. Use as patient literature, handouts at presentations, and aids for promoting your mental health practice.

- ❏ Adult Client Education Handout Planner ..................................................... 978-0-471-20232-5 / $60.00
- ❏ Child and Adolescent Client Education Handout Planner .......................... 978-0-471-20233-2 / $60.00
- ❏ Couples and Family Client Education Handout Planner ............................. 978-0-471-20234-9 / $60.00

Name _____
Affiliation _____
Address _____
City/State/Zip _____
Phone/Fax _____
E-mail _____
❏ Check enclosed  ❏ Visa  ❏ MasterCard  ❏ American Express
Card # _____
Expiration Date _____
Signature _____

*Add $5 shipping for first book, $3 for each additional book. Please add your local sales tax to all orders. Prices subject to change without notice.

**To order by phone in the US:**
Call toll free 1-877-762-2974

**Online:** www.practiceplanners.wiley.com

**Mail this order form to:**
Wiley, Attn: Customer Care
10475 Crosspoint Blvd.
Indianapolis, IN 46256

# Group Therapy
# Homework Planner

## Wiley PracticePlanners® Series

### Treatment Planners

*The Complete Adult Psychotherapy Treatment Planner, Fifth Edition*
*The Child Psychotherapy Treatment Planner, Fifth Edition*
*The Adolescent Psychotherapy Treatment Planner, Fifth Edition*
*The Addiction Treatment Planner, Fifth Edition*
*The Continuum of Care Treatment Planner*
*The Couples Psychotherapy Treatment Planner, with DSM-5 Updates, Second Edition*
*The Employee Assistance Treatment Planner*
*The Pastoral Counseling Treatment Planner*
*The Older Adult Psychotherapy treatment Planner with DSM-5 Updates, Second Edition*
*The Behavioral Medicine Treatment Planner*
*The Group Therapy Treatment Planner*
*The Gay and Lesbian Psychotherapy Treatment Planner*
*The Family Therapy Treatment Planner, with DSM-5 Updates, Second Edition*
*The Severe and Persistent Mental Illness Treatment Planner, with DSM-5 Updates, Second Edition*
*The Mental Retardation and Developmental Disability Treatment Planner*
*The Social Work and Human Services Treatment Planner*
*The Crisis Counseling and Traumatic Events Treatments Planner, with DSM-5 Updates, Second Edition*
*The Personality Disorders Treatments Planner*
*The Rehabilitation Psychology Treatment Planner*
*The Special Education Treatment planner*
*The Juvenile Justice and Residential Care Treatment Planner*
*The School Counseling and School Social Work Treatment Planner, with DSM-5 Updates, Second Edition*
*The Sexual Abuse Victim and Sexual Offender Treatment Planner*
*The Probation and Parole Treatment Planner*
*The Psychopharmacology Treatment Planner*
*The Speech-Language Pathology Treatment Planner*
*The Suicide and Homicide Treatment Planner*
*The College Student Counseling Treatment Planner*
*The Parenting Skills Treatment Planner*
*The Early Childhood Intervention Treatment Planner*
*The Co-Occurring Disorders Treatment Planner*
*The Complete Women's Psychotherapy Treatment Planner*
*The Veterans and Active Duty Military Psychotherapy Treatment Planner, with DSM-5 Updates*

### Progress Notes Planners

*The Child Psychotherapy Progress Notes Planner, Fifth Edition*
*The Adolescent Psychotherapy Progress Notes Planner, Fifth Edition*
*The Adult Psychotherapy Progress Notes Planner, Fifth Edition*
*The Addiction Progress Notes Planner, Fifth Edition*
*The Severe and Persistent Mental Illness Progress Notes Planner, Second Edition*
*The Couples Psychotherapy Progress Notes Planner, Second Edition*
*The Family Therapy Progress Notes Planner, Second Edition*
*The Veterans and Active Duty Military Psychotherapy Progress Notes Planner*

### Homework Planners

*Couples Therapy Homework Planner, Second Edition*
*Family Therapy Homework Planner, Second Edition*
*Grief Counseling Homework Planner*
*Group Therapy Homework Planner*
*Divorce Counseling Homework Planner*
*School Counseling and School Social Work Homework Planner, Second Edition*
*Child Therapy Activity and Homework Planner*
*Addiction Treatment Homework Planner, Fifth Edition*
*Adolescent Psychotherapy Homework Planner, Fifth Edition*
*Adult Psychotherapy Homework Planner, Fifth Edition*
*Child Psychotherapy Homework Planner, Fifth Edition*
*Parenting Skills Homework Planner*
*Veterans and Active Duty Military Psychotherapy Homework Planner*

### Client Education Handout Planners

*Adult Client Education Handout Planner*
*Child and Adolescent Client Education Handout Planner*
*Couples and Family Client Education Handout Planner*

### Complete Planners

*The Complete Depression Treatment and Homework Planner*
*The Complete Anxiety Treatment and Homework Planner*

**Wiley PracticePlanners**

Arthur E. Jongsma, Jr., Series Editor

# Group Therapy Homework Planner

*Louis J. Bevilacqua*

WILEY

> **A NOTE TO THE READER**
> This book has been electronically reproduced from digital information stored at John Wiley & Sons, Inc. We are pleased that the use of this new technology will enable us to keep works of enduring scholarly value in print as long as there is a reasonable demand for them. The content of this book is identical to previous printings.

Copyright © 2002 by John Wiley & Sons. All rights reserved.

Published simultaneously in Canada.

No part of this publication may be reproduced, stored in a retrieval system or transmitted in any form or by any means, electronic, mechanical, photocopying, recording, scanning or otherwise, except as permitted under Sections 107 or 108 of the 1976 United States Copyright Act, without either the prior written permission of the Publisher, or authorization through payment of the appropriate per-copy fee to the Copyright Clearance Center, 222 Rosewood Drive, Danvers, MA 01923, (978) 750-8400, fax (978) 750-4470. Requests to the Publisher for permission should be addressed to the Permissions Department, John Wiley & Sons, Inc., 111 River Street, Hoboken, NJ 07030, (201) 748-6011, fax (201) 748-6008.

This publication is designed to provide accurate and authoritative information in regard to the subject matter covered. It is sold with the understanding that the publisher is not engaged in rendering professional services. If legal, accounting, medical, psychological or any other expert assistance is required, the services of a competent professional person should be sought.

Designations used by companies to distinguish their products are often claimed as trademarks. In all instances where John Wiley & Sons, Inc., is aware of a claim, the product names appear in initial capital or all capital letters. Readers, however, should contact the appropriate companies for more complete information regarding trademarks and registration.

> **Note about Photocopy Rights**
> The publisher grants purchasers permission to reproduce handouts from this book for professional use with their clients.

*Library of Congress Cataloging-in-Publication Data:*

Bevilacqua, Louis.
   Group therapy homework planner / Louis J. Bevilacqua.
     p. cm. — (Practice planners series)
   ISBN 978-1-119-23065-6 (pbk)
    1. Group psychotherapy—Problems, exercises, etc.  I. Title.  II. Practice planners.

RC488 .B474 2001
616.89'152—dc21
                                2001045390

I dedicate this book to all those children, adolescents, and adults who have taught me the value of group therapy and the benefits of therapeutic homework assignments.

—LOUIS J. BEVILACQUA

# CONTENTS

| | |
|---|---|
| **Wiley Practice*Planners*® Series Preface** | xiii |
| Introduction | xv |
| | |
| SECTION I—Adult Children of Alcoholics | 1 |
|     Exercise I.A     What's My Role? | 3 |
|     Exercise I.B     What Can I Control? What Do I Need? | 6 |
|     Exercise I.C     We're Not Supposed to Talk about That! | 9 |
| | |
| SECTION II—Agoraphobia/Panic | 10 |
|     Exercise II.A     When Is This Going to Happen? | 12 |
|     Exercise II.B     Breaking My Panic Cycle | 14 |
|     Exercise II.C     Facing Fears—Part One | 17 |
|     Exercise II.D     Facing Fears—Part Two | 20 |
| | |
| SECTION III—Anger Control Problems | 22 |
|     Exercise III.A     Anger Log | 24 |
|     Exercise III.B     Is It Anger or Aggression? | 27 |
|     Exercise III.C     Go Blow Out Some Candles | 31 |
|     Exercise III.D     My Safe Place | 33 |
| | |
| SECTION IV—Anxiety | 34 |
|     Exercise IV.A     What Happens When I Feel Anxious? | 36 |
|     Exercise IV.B     What Else Can I Say or Do? | 39 |
|     Exercise IV.C     Beating Self-Defeating Beliefs | 42 |
| | |
| SECTION V—Assertiveness Deficit | 44 |
|     Exercise V.A     Is It Passive, Aggressive, or Assertive? | 46 |
|     Exercise V.B     It's Okay to Be Assertive | 51 |

## SECTION VI—Bulimia ........ 53

| | | |
|---|---|---|
| Exercise VI.A | Am I Hungry? | 55 |
| Exercise VI.B | I Need to Get Control | 59 |
| Exercise VI.C | What Am I Thinking? | 62 |
| Exercise VI.D | Is It Good Food or Bad Food? Should It Matter That Much? | 65 |

## SECTION VII—Caregiver Burnout ........ 67

| | | |
|---|---|---|
| Exercise VII.A | Being a Caregiver Makes Me Feel . . . | 69 |
| Exercise VII.B | This Is for Me and That's Okay | 71 |
| Exercise VII.C | What Drawer Does This Belong In? | 74 |

## SECTION VIII—Chemical Dependence ........ 76

| | | |
|---|---|---|
| Exercise VIII.A | I Use Because . . . | 78 |
| Exercise VIII.B | What to Do Instead of Using | 82 |
| Exercise VIII.C | My Road Map to Recovery | 86 |

## SECTION IX—Child Sexual Molestation ........ 91

| | | |
|---|---|---|
| Exercise IX.A | This Is What Happened | 93 |
| Exercise IX.B | This Is What I Did | 96 |
| Exercise IX.C | I'm Changing the Way I Think | 100 |
| Exercise IX.D | Stop! Rewind! And Start Again | 103 |

## SECTION X—Chronic Pain ........ 105

| | | |
|---|---|---|
| Exercise X.A | Aah! Relief, Written and Directed by _____ (Write in Your Name) | 107 |
| Exercise X.B | I Can Get through This | 110 |

## SECTION XI—Codependence ........ 112

| | | |
|---|---|---|
| Exercise XI.A | I'm Not in Kansas Anymore | 114 |
| Exercise XI.B | I Feel . . . | 117 |

## SECTION XII—Depression ........ 119

| | | |
|---|---|---|
| Exercise XII.A | What Do Others Value about Me? | 121 |
| Exercise XII.B | My Feelings Journal | 123 |
| Exercise XII.C | Taking Charge of Your Thoughts | 126 |
| Exercise XII.D | There's Always a Sunrise | 130 |

| | | |
|---|---|---|
| SECTION XIII—Domestic Violence Offenders | | 131 |
| Exercise XIII.A | When Do I Need a Break? | 133 |
| Exercise XIII.B | Now Is When I Need a Break | 136 |
| Exercise XIII.C | I Can Have Feelings, Too | 138 |
| | | |
| SECTION XIV—Domestic Violence Survivors | | 140 |
| Exercise XIV.A | What I Give and What I Get | 142 |
| Exercise XIV.B | What If . . . ? | 144 |
| Exercise XIV.C | Thoughts about This Relationship | 147 |
| | | |
| SECTION XV—Grief/Loss Unresolved | | 148 |
| Exercise XV.A | Farewell, until We Meet Again | 150 |
| Exercise XV.B | Moving On | 153 |
| | | |
| SECTION XVI—HIV/AIDS | | 156 |
| Exercise XVI.A | How Am I Doing? | 158 |
| Exercise XVI.B | Why Me? | 161 |
| | | |
| SECTION XVII—Incest Offenders—Adult | | 164 |
| Exercise XVII.A | Through the Eyes of a Child | 166 |
| Exercise XVII.B | Stress and Trigger Journal | 170 |
| Exercise XVII.C | My Letter of Apology | 172 |
| | | |
| SECTION XVIII—Incest Survivors—Adult | | 173 |
| Exercise XVIII.A | My Story | 175 |
| Exercise XVIII.B | What I Need to Tell You | 179 |
| | | |
| SECTION XIX—Infertility | | 180 |
| Exercise XIX.A | Being a Parent Means . . . | 182 |
| Exercise XIX.B | What If We Have a Child Some Other Way? | 185 |
| | | |
| SECTION XX—Parenting Problems | | 188 |
| Exercise XX.A | Working from the Same Page | 190 |
| Exercise XX.B | What's the Message I Am Giving? What's the Message I Mean? | 194 |
| Exercise XX.C | Compliments Jar | 198 |
| Exercise XX.D | What Are My Choices? | 202 |

xii CONTENTS

| | | |
|---|---|---|
| SECTION XXI—Phobias—Specific/Social | | 205 |
| Exercise XXI.A | I Can Picture It | 207 |
| Exercise XXI.B | How Does This Happen? | 209 |
| Exercise XXI.C | Let's Float with It | 212 |
| Exercise XXI.D | I Can Do This | 215 |
| SECTION XXII—Rape Survivors | | 217 |
| Exercise XXII.A | Sharing My Story | 219 |
| Exercise XXII.B | Changing My Faulty Thinking | 222 |
| Exercise XXII.C | What I Feel and What I Think | 225 |
| SECTION XXIII—Separation and Divorce | | 226 |
| Exercise XXIII.A | Talking to the Children | 228 |
| Exercise XXIII.B | We Need to Agree | 231 |
| Exercise XXIII.C | Saying Good-bye and Saying Hello | 235 |
| SECTION XXIV—Shyness | | 238 |
| Exercise XXIV.A | Three Key Ingredients to Positive Social Interactions | 240 |
| Exercise XXIV.B | What Comes after "Hi"? | 242 |
| SECTION XXV—Single Parents | | 246 |
| Exercise XXV.A | Single Parenting—Pro or Con? | 248 |
| Exercise XXV.B | What Do I Do Now? | 250 |
| SECTION XXVI—Toxic Parent Survivors | | 253 |
| Exercise XXVI.A | I Am Getting Rid of These Old Tapes—Part One | 255 |
| Exercise XXVI.B | I Am Getting Rid of These Old Tapes—Part Two | 258 |
| SECTION XXVII—Type-A Stress | | 261 |
| Exercise XXVII.A | Where's My Tension? | 263 |
| Exercise XXVII.B | When I Feel Tension/Stress I Can . . . | 266 |
| SECTION XXVIII—Vocational Stress | | 269 |
| Exercise XXVIII.A | What Else Can I Do to Make Things Better? | 271 |
| Exercise XXVIII.B | How I Will Get What I Want | 275 |
| About the Author | | 277 |
| About the Downloadable Assignments | | 279 |

# WILEY PRACTICE*PLANNERS*® SERIES PREFACE

Accountability is an important dimension of the practice of psychotherapy. Treatment programs, public agencies, clinics, and practitioners must justify and document their treatment plans to outside review entities in order to be reimbursed for services. The books and software in the wiley Practice*Planners*® series are designed to help practitioners fulfill these documentation requirements efficiently and professionally.

The wiley Practice*Planners*® series includes a wide array of treatment planning books including not only the original *Complete Adult Psychotherapy Treatment Planner*, *Child Psychotherapy Treatment Planner*, and *Adolescent Psychotherapy Treatment Planner*, all now in their fifth editions, but also *Treatment Planners* targeted to specialty areas of practice, including:

- Addictions
- Co-occurring disorders
- Behavioral medicine
- College students
- Couples therapy
- Crisis counseling
- Early childhood education
- Employee assistance
- Family therapy
- Gays and lesbians
- Group therapy
- Juvenile justice and residential care
- Mental retardation and developmental disability
- Neuropsychology
- Older adults
- Parenting skills
- Pastoral counseling
- Personality disorders
- Probation and parole
- Psychopharmacology
- Rehabilitation psychology
- School counseling and school social work
- Severe and persistent mental illness
- Sexual abuse victims and offenders

- Social work and human services
- Special education
- Speech-language pathology
- Suicide and homicide risk assessment
- Veterans and active military duty
- Women's issues

In addition, there are three branches of companion books that can be used in conjunction with the *Treatment Planners*, or on their own:

- ***Progress Notes Planners*** provide a menu of progress statements that elaborate on the client's symptom presentation and the provider's therapeutic intervention. Each *Progress Notes Planner* statement is directly integrated with the behavioral definitions and therapeutic interventions from its companion *Treatment Planner*.

- ***Homework Planners*** include homework assignments designed around each presenting problem (such as anxiety, depression, substance use, anger control problems, eating disorders, or panic disorder) that is the focus of a chapter in its corresponding *Treatment Planner*.

- ***Client Education Handout Planners*** provide brochures and handouts to help educate and inform clients on presenting problems and mental health issues, as well as life skills techniques. The handouts are included online for easy printing from your computer and are ideal for use in waiting rooms, at presentations, as newsletters, or as information for clients struggling with mental illness issues. The topics covered by these handouts correspond to the presenting problems in the *Treatment Planners*.

Adjunctive books, such as *The Psychotherapy Documentation Primer* and *The Clinical Documentation Sourcebook*, contain forms and resources to aid the clinician in mental health practice management.

The goal of our series is to provide practitioners with the resources they need in order to provide high quality care in the era of accountability. To put it simply: We seek to help you spend more time on patients, and less time on paperwork.

ARTHUR E. JONGSMA, JR.
*Grand Rapids, Michigan*

# INTRODUCTION

Congratulations on deciding to purchase this book. This is probably one of the best investments that you can make, particularly in light of the ever-increasing need for treatment planning and documentation in your clinical practice.

Although all therapeutic modalities do not utilize homework assignments in the same way, the majority of them do find it necessary to recommend assignments as a means of following through with the facilitation of change. In fact, homework assignments are probably one of the main ingredients to solidifying change in the psychotherapeutic process. This is most likely due to the fact that a significant portion of change actually occurs once the clients leave the therapist's office.

Thus, homework assignments help the therapy gel because the majority of clients' time is spent outside of the therapeutic hour. This is true now more than ever in an age where increasing emphasis has been placed on short-term psychotherapy and the need for structured treatment and independent assignments. Homework that is specifically germane to the content of the therapy session is essential in assuring change. It is with this philosophy that I offer the contents of this homework planner for the contemporary group therapist.

The specific homework assignments in this text have been specially tailored to help the group therapist guide group members in achieving lasting change. They are closely keyed to the topics covered in the adjoining *Group Psychotherapy Treatment Planner* (Paleg and Jongsma, 2000) and have been designed to be user friendly with a number of contemporary modalities of group therapy.

A concerted effort has been made to be as comprehensive as possible in order to provide you with an abundance of exercises that you may implement in treatment regardless of your particular approach.

## USING THIS BOOK TO ITS FULLEST

First and foremost, these homework assignments are grouped under presenting problems, which correspond to the *Group Psychotherapy Treatment Planner* (Paleg and Jongsma, 2000). These problems are typical of the types that individuals seek group therapy treatment for.

Each chapter begins with a note to the therapist on how to suggest the use of a particular exercise. It should be noted that this is not a self-help book, but rather is designed to be used by professionally trained therapists as therapeutic prescriptions for bolstering techniques and facilitating change with group members. It is, therefore, only to be used under the guidance of a professionally trained therapist.

Each homework assignment is easy to reproduce and may be distributed at the beginning or end of group therapy sessions. Professionals using the exercises should feel free to embellish or modify the homework assignment in order to fit the particular case with which they are working. Groups are not all alike, nor are the individual members. Therefore, alterations and modifications become necessary and may be most effective if made to fit each group/individual member.

It is also recommended that these homework assignments be used as a stepping stone to generate your own homework assignments by simply inserting the disk into your computer and altering it as you see fit, making substantial or minor changes.

Assignments are more likely to be followed if professionals work along with group members to develop them, collaboratively using their input as a key ingredient in the homework assignment. What is important is that the homework assignment becomes tailored and pertinent to the specific problems that the group is experiencing.

Above all, the group therapist should use his/her clinical judgment when implementing such homework assignments. Homework, obviously, is not for everyone, and it is only the clinical professional who can determine the right time and place to make suggestions for homework assignments.

It is very important that you read through the entire contents and familiarize yourself with each assignment before actually suggesting it to group members. This will be very important during your initial use of this book until you become familiar with the types of reactions and results that are obtained as a result of the assignments.

## IMPLEMENTING THE ASSIGNMENTS

In implementing these assignments, you should keep a number of things in mind. First, it is important to think about how you wish to suggest the use of assignments during the course of therapy and at what point in the treatment process would be a good time to intervene. This, of course, varies and will be left up to your clinical judgment. Once you decide to utilize the assignments, then it is suggested that you use your own style in approaching your clients. Before ending the session, be sure to review the assignment with them so that they understand the reasoning for doing the assignment, as well as what specifically they are to do. To clarify and to increase the likelihood of your clients following through, have them repeat why they are agreeing to the assignment. Make sure they believe it to be a good idea and that they understand the benefits. When you encounter individuals who do not agree or refuse, you must use your clinical judgment to determine how much to push and confront. The more agreement that you have among group members about trying the assignment, the more likely the assignments are to be successful.

Follow-up on the results is obviously very important and might best be accomplished by making this a part of the group agenda or routine. By following up on the results of homeworks, the message conveyed is that these assignments are important. This also conveys a sense of accountability among group members. Often, when a group has achieved some cohesiveness, group members will expect that all members work together, including completing homework assignments. When individuals do not, it allows for the group process of the working stage to become activated.

Sometimes individuals do not complete assignments because they're not sure what to do or why. In addition, sometimes it is as simple as the terminology used. Some individuals have a negative view of homework due to bad experience during their school-age years. You might be able to avoid this problem by referring to the assignments as a *task* or *experiment*.

Whenever homework, tasks, or experiments are not completed, it is important to figure out why. In doing so, it is best to keep an open mind. Perhaps you were not clear in communicating the task or the reasons for doing it, as well as the benefits. Perhaps you assigned it during the last minute of the group time so there was not enough time to process it. One of the most significant factors to address is whether the task was decided on in a collaborative fashion. The more you are able to convey that the group members have a voice in what they do, the more cooperation you will tend to receive.

Last, the type and nature of the assignment may contribute to some reasons for resistance or failure. If this is the case, perhaps an alternative assignment may be in order.

It is my hope that this book will prove to be an invaluable resource for you in your challenging work with groups. Above all, it is also my goal that the following exercises may help you to expand your repertoire in the same vein that it may help the individuals in your groups grow as well.

Louis J. Bevilacqua

## Section I

# ADULT CHILDREN OF ALCOHOLICS

Therapist's Overview

# WHAT'S MY ROLE?

## GOALS OF THE EXERCISE

1. Develop a better understanding of one's own needs and ways to meet them.
2. Recognize your own behaviors and thoughts that create inner conflicts and that interfere in relationships.
3. Replace negative, self-defeating thoughts and behaviors with more positive self-adaptive thoughts and behaviors.

## ADDITIONAL HOMEWORK THAT MAY BE APPLICABLE TO CLIENTS WHO ARE CHILDREN OF ALCOHOLICS

- Anxiety             Beating Self-Defeating Beliefs        Page 42
- Codependence        I'm Not in Kansas Anymore             Page 114
- Depression          There's Always a Sunrise              Page 130

## ADDITIONAL PROBLEMS IN WHICH THIS EXERCISE MAY BE USEFUL

- Codependence

## SUGGESTIONS FOR PROCESSING THIS EXERCISE WITH THE CLIENT

When children grow up in an alcoholic home, they tend to learn to fear emotional abandonment, have trouble trusting others, and are unable to express their own feelings, wishes, or needs. As a result, they will learn to identify with a particular role. This role, frequently, follows them into adulthood. In a group setting, members can be extremely helpful in pointing out when others are acting out their assigned roles. The goal, however, is for individual members to improve their self-monitoring skills and recognize it themselves. They then need to learn ways to change. The following exercise is designed to help group members identify and recognize when they are engaging in such roles, as well as what to do about it.

Exercise I.A

# WHAT'S MY ROLE?

The following exercise is designed to help you identify when you are acting out a role and what you can do to change.

1. Describe the characteristics of many adult children of alcoholics.

2. Pick out characteristics with which you tend to identify most.

3. Are you more like the *placater, adjuster, responsible one,* or the *acting-out child*? Why do you think so?

4. Describe times when you have engaged in these behaviors.

Exercise I.A

5. Keep track this week of times when you engage in such role behavior and the thoughts and feelings that occur during such times.

| Behavior | Day/Time | Thought | Feeling |
|---|---|---|---|
| | | | |
| | | | |
| | | | |
| | | | |
| | | | |
| | | | |
| | | | |

6. Pick two or three of the situations in no. 5 and describe what you wanted to do or say but didn't.

_____
_____
_____
_____

7. Review the "Thoughts" column in no. 5. For each negative thought, write a more adaptive and positive thought.

| Negative/self-defeating thought | Positive thought |
|---|---|
| | |
| | |
| | |
| | |
| | |
| | |
| | |

*Therapist's Overview*

# WHAT CAN I CONTROL? WHAT DO I NEED?

## GOALS OF THE EXERCISE

1. Recognize situations in which you do have control and those in which you do not.
2. Identify feelings associated with situations in which you do have control and those in which you do not.
3. Develop a sense of boundaries and ways to take care of oneself.

## ADDITIONAL HOMEWORK THAT MAY BE APPLICABLE TO CLIENTS WHO ARE CHILDREN OF ALCOHOLICS

- Anxiety — Beating Self-Defeating Beliefs — Page 42
- Codependence — I'm Not in Kansas Anymore — Page 114
- Depression — There's Always a Sunrise — Page 130

## ADDITIONAL PROBLEMS IN WHICH THIS EXERCISE MAY BE USEFUL

- Anger Control Problems
- Codependence

## SUGGESTIONS FOR PROCESSING THIS EXERCISE WITH THE CLIENT

This exercise is designed to help individuals break away from the pattern of trying to please others so much that they have forgotten about themselves and their own needs. Control is a central issue with this problem. By helping individuals figure out the process of how they end up doing so much for others, they can also learn how to start accepting what they can control and what they don't have to try to control.

Exercise I.B

# WHAT CAN I CONTROL? WHAT DO I NEED?

If you are tired of trying to please others so much that you have forgotten about who you are, this exercise can help. Learning what you can control and what you cannot is a key ingredient to changing this pattern.

1. Make a list of at least 10 activities that you do for yourself (e.g., take a bubble bath, get your nails done, go out to dinner, etc.).
   A. _____
   B. _____
   C. _____
   D. _____
   E. _____
   F. _____
   G. _____
   H. _____
   I. _____
   J. _____

2. Keep track of what you do. Was that for me or for someone else? Ask yourself if you were in control.

| Behavior | Me or someone else? | Was I in control? |
|----------|---------------------|-------------------|
|          |                     |                   |
|          |                     |                   |
|          |                     |                   |
|          |                     |                   |
|          |                     |                   |
|          |                     |                   |

Exercise I.B

3. Review your list and describe how you felt in each situation.

_____
_____
_____
_____
_____

Often, it is helpful to evaluate our behavior to see if we are being true to ourselves. Sometimes, we find that we do things either out of habit or a need to avoid conflict. For this next part, the goal is to begin challenging the reasons for your behavior.

4. Keep track of times when others ask you to do something and you do it despite really not wanting to. Be as honest with yourself as you can.

| Behavior | If I did not do this, what would happen? |
|---|---|
| | |
| | |
| | |
| | |
| | |
| | |

5. Ask two or three others if they agree with your answer to "what would happen?"

6. In each of the preceding situations, describe what you were hoping to control (e.g., "I didn't want them to think badly of me").

_____
_____
_____
_____

7. Try turning someone down the next time they ask you to do something. Describe what happens.

_____
_____
_____
_____

Therapist's Overview

# WE'RE NOT SUPPOSED TO TALK ABOUT THAT!

## GOALS OF THE EXERCISE

1. Members give voice to the feelings and thoughts that they've held in because of the "Don't talk" rule in the family.
2. Members acknowledge the feelings that are associated with the times when they kept quiet or broke the rule.
3. Members recognize how they continue the "Don't talk" rule nowadays.

## ADDITIONAL HOMEWORK THAT MAY BE APPLICABLE TO CLIENTS WHO ARE CHILDREN OF ALCOHOLICS

- Anxiety            Beating Self-Defeating Beliefs        Page 42
- Codependence       I'm Not in Kansas Anymore             Page 114
- Depression         There's Always a Sunrise              Page 130

## ADDITIONAL PROBLEMS IN WHICH THIS EXERCISE MAY BE USEFUL

- Codependence
- Incest

## SUGGESTIONS FOR PROCESSING THIS EXERCISE WITH THE CLIENT

In most situations, children of alcoholics grew up with the family rule of "Don't talk about it." Secrecy is a key factor to any kind of abuse continuing, whether it be alcoholism, drug abuse, or child abuse. Living by this rule teaches children to disregard feelings of uncomfortableness ("This doesn't feel right but no one talks about it. I guess I shouldn't feel this way"). This can continue into adulthood and lead to many adults having difficulty with speaking up for themselves and taking care of having their own needs met.

Exercise I.C

# WE'RE NOT SUPPOSED TO TALK ABOUT THAT!

How many times have you swallowed your feelings and thoughts? Want to stop? Complete the following exercise as a way of learning to have a voice for your thoughts and feelings. P.S.—You can talk about it!

1. Recall and record times when you felt uneasy in your family.

   _____
   _____
   _____
   _____

2. What feelings did you have back then? What feelings do you have now as you are thinking about it?

   _____
   _____
   _____
   _____

3. Write down what you were saying to yourself but rarely, if ever, said out loud. Or think about what you would say now.

   _____
   _____
   _____
   _____

4. During this week, pay attention to times when you feel as if "I can't or shouldn't talk." Write about these situations, and your fears or other feelings.

   _____
   _____
   _____
   _____

5. In your next group session, discuss your experiences, thoughts, and feelings.

# Section II

# AGORAPHOBIA/PANIC

**Therapist's Overview**

# WHEN IS THIS GOING TO HAPPEN?

## GOALS OF THE EXERCISE

1. To learn what happens when panic strikes.
2. To develop more control over the fear of panic attacks.
3. To reduce the incidence of panic attacks.

## ADDITIONAL HOMEWORK THAT MAY BE APPLICABLE TO AGORAPHOBIA/PANIC

- Anxiety                      What Happens When I Feel Anxious?    Page 36
- Depression                   My Feelings Journal                  Page 123
- Phobias—Specific/Social      Let's Float with It                  Page 212

## ADDITIONAL PROBLEMS IN WHICH THIS EXERCISE MAY BE USEFUL

- Anger Control Problems
- Phobias—Specific/Social

## SUGGESTIONS FOR PROCESSING THIS EXERCISE WITH THE CLIENT

Agoraphobia and panic attacks can be devastating. The fear of being panic-stricken is overwhelming. Individuals need to learn the triggers to panic and how to regain control of their lives. Explain to the group the relationship between thoughts, feelings, and behaviors and the role of avoidance as a maintenance factor. The following exercise will help group members become familiar with their pattern of avoidance based on their fears. Before giving this exercise, you may want to introduce or review diaphragmatic breathing.

Exercise II.A

# WHEN IS THIS GOING TO HAPPEN?

Wouldn't it be great to be able to predict and change the circumstances around when a panic attack is going to occur? You will be able to do this soon. One of the first steps, however, is being able to identify when it has happened in the past and what the circumstances were at that time. This exercise will help you to identify those circumstances.

Think of the last time when you had a panic attack or feared that you were going to have one.

1. Where were you?
   _____

2. Who was nearby?
   _____

3. Describe what was happening before you started feeling anxious.
   _____
   _____

4. Were you breathing up in your chest and throat or down in your belly?
   _____

5. How fast were you breathing? ____ A little fast ____ Somewhat fast ____ Very fast

6. List any other physical sensations you felt (e.g., sweating, dizziness, shakiness, nausea).
   _____
   _____

7. What were some of your thoughts (e.g., "I'm going to panic," "I can't _____ ," "I'm going to have a heart attack")?
   _____
   _____
   _____

8. What did you do (e.g., sat on the couch and turned on the television, had a cigarette)?
   _____
   _____
   _____

Therapist's Overview

# BREAKING MY PANIC CYCLE

## GOALS OF THE EXERCISE

1. Reduce the incidence of panic attacks.
2. Take control over panic symptoms and learn ways to redirect and eliminate them.
3. Replace anxiety-provoking thoughts with more adaptive and self-affirming thoughts.
4. Replace avoidant and anxiety-reinforcing behaviors with assertive and anxiety-reducing behaviors.

## ADDITIONAL HOMEWORK THAT MAY BE APPLICABLE TO AGORAPHOBIA/PANIC

- Anxiety                 What Happens When I Feel Anxious?      Page 36
- Depression             My Feelings Journal                     Page 123
- Phobias—Specific/Social    Let's Float with It                       Page 212

## ADDITIONAL PROBLEMS IN WHICH THIS EXERCISE MAY BE USEFUL

- Anger Control Problems
- Phobias—Specific/Social

## SUGGESTIONS FOR PROCESSING THIS EXERCISE WITH THE CLIENT

This exercise should follow the "When Is This Going to Happen?" assignment, in which each group member learned the surrounding circumstances to when he/she experiences panic. In the current exercise, each group member will be applying the information from that exercise to understand what his/her panic cycle is. The member will then be able to change and break that cycle.

Exercise II.B

# BREAKING MY PANIC CYCLE

Apply the information that you learned from the exercise, "When Is This Going to Happen?," to determine your panic cycle. The panic cycle essentially involves three steps that follow an emotional or physical trigger to anxiety/stress. When you experience stress or are faced with having to do something with which you are uncomfortable, anxiety results. This is when the panic cycle begins. Step 1 develops after the experience of a stressor. This step involves the physical sensations (e.g., shortness of breath, trembling) that you experience. Step 2 is the negative and catastrophic thoughts that go through your mind. Step 3 is the avoidance behavior you engage in to decrease the physical symptoms and negative thoughts or the panic attack that result. This exercise is designed to help you break that panic cycle.

1. List the emotional or physical trigger(s) that lead you to feel stress/anxiety.

   _____
   _____
   _____
   _____
   _____
   _____

Over the next week, when these or other emotional/physical triggers occur, use the following chart to keep track of what you do (physically and cognitively) and what you can do differently.

2. Physical sensations of anxiety (e.g., dizziness, trembling, shortness of breath) | What I can do (e.g., deep breathing, visualization, journal)

Exercise II.B

3. Negative thought (e.g., "I'm going to have a heart attack")

   _____
   _____
   _____
   _____
   _____

   Alternative thought (e.g., "I've survived this before, I will survive it now")

   _____
   _____
   _____
   _____
   _____

4. Avoidance behavior (e.g., Sat on couch and smoked a cigarette)

   _____
   _____
   _____
   _____
   _____

   Challenging behavior (e.g., review list of "What I can do")

   _____
   _____
   _____
   _____
   _____

5. Result (e.g., "I stayed home alone, and my friends went on without me")

   _____
   _____
   _____
   _____
   _____

   Result (e.g., "I took charge and reduced my anxiety")

   _____
   _____
   _____
   _____
   _____

Therapist's Overview

# FACING FEARS—PART ONE

## GOALS OF THE EXERCISE

1. Increase feelings of power over anxiety and fears.
2. Develop a plan of desensitizing yourself to your fears.

## ADDITIONAL HOMEWORK THAT MAY BE APPLICABLE TO AGORAPHOBIA/PANIC

- Anxiety — What Happens When I Feel Anxious? — Page 36
- Depression — My Feelings Journal — Page 123
- Phobias—Specific/Social — I Can Picture It — Page 207
- Phobias—Specific/Social — Let's Float with It — Page 212

## ADDITIONAL PROBLEMS IN WHICH THIS EXERCISE MAY BE USEFUL

- Anger Control Problems
- Anxiety
- Phobias—Specific/Social
- Shyness

## SUGGESTIONS FOR PROCESSING THIS EXERCISE WITH THE CLIENT

Group members need to be able to apply the strategies that they have learned from the previous exercises to any other anxiety-provoking situation or experience. Talk to them first about the top 5 to 10 situations that create anxiety for them. Have them rate each situation on a personal anxiety rating scale (0 to 10). Ask them to list the situations from lowest to highest and explain that this is their anxiety hierarchy. Explain that they will need to utilize their skills of deep breathing and visualization to face each situation and reduce the anxiety rating level. Review with them the concepts and principles of systematic desensitization. After practicing this in the group, assign them the following exercise.

Exercise II.C

# FACING FEARS—PART ONE

In certain situations, anxiety is a very positive emotion. For example, anxiety keeps you aware of when you need to pay your bills, or to dress nice, or to study so that you can do well on a test. When you experience too much anxiety, you can begin to feel trapped. To set yourself free of anxiety, you must learn to face your fears. With the help of your support network and the skills that you have learned in your group sessions (i.e., deep breathing and visualization), you cannot only face your fears, but also overcome them. The following exercise is designed to help you get started.

1. Construct a hierarchy of situations and experiences from least to most anxiety provoking. Rate each situation or experience on a personal anxiety scale (0 to 10). Each situation or experience may need to be broken down into steps. For example, one anxiety situation might be walking around the block. The first step may be picturing yourself opening the front door. Step 2 would be picturing yourself spending a few minutes outside on the front step. Step 3 could be imagining yourself walking to the sidewalk. Step 4 could be imagining yourself walking to the corner. Step 5 could be imagining yourself walking halfway around the block. Step 6 could be picturing yourself walking all the way around the block. Constructing your hierarchy should be done in-group and reviewed by your therapist before you try it at home.

| Anxiety-provoking situation | Rating |
|---|---|
| 10. _____ | _____ |
| 9. _____ | _____ |
| 8. _____ | _____ |
| 7. _____ | _____ |
| 6. _____ | _____ |
| 5. _____ | _____ |
| 4. _____ | _____ |
| 3. _____ | _____ |
| 2. _____ | _____ |
| 1. _____ | _____ |

2. Picture level 1 of your hierarchy. Describe the situation to yourself. Imagine it as vividly as you can. What are you thinking, doing, and feeling? Who is with you? What are they doing? Once you have the picture in your mind and can fully imagine the situation, start to practice your coping skills of deep breathing, visualization, and positive self-talk. Continue this until your rating of this situation decreases to zero or to no higher than one.
3. Do this every day, and do not move on to the next level in the hierarchy until the lower level no longer produces a personal anxiety rating above one.
4. Journal about your attempts each day and discuss in your next group session.

Therapist's Overview

# FACING FEARS—PART TWO

## GOALS OF THE EXERCISE

1. Increase feelings of power over anxiety and fears.
2. Be able to confront and overcome your fears.

## ADDITIONAL HOMEWORK THAT MAY BE APPLICABLE TO AGORAPHOBIA/PANIC

- Anxiety — What Happens When I Feel Anxious? — Page 36
- Depression — My Feelings Journal — Page 123
- Phobias—Specific/Social — I Can Picture It — Page 207
- Phobias—Specific/Social — Let's Float with It — Page 212

## ADDITIONAL PROBLEMS IN WHICH THIS EXERCISE MAY BE USEFUL

- Anger Control Problems
- Phobias—Specific/Social
- Shyness

## SUGGESTIONS FOR PROCESSING THIS EXERCISE WITH THE CLIENT

This exercise is an extension of the previous one. The difference is that this exercise is asking the group members to apply the skills of deep breathing, positive self-talk, visualization, and so forth to face and overcome their fears.

Exercise II.D

# FACING FEARS—PART TWO

This exercise is an extension of "Facing Fears—Part I." Instead of imagining the fears in your hierarchy, this time you will be facing and confronting each fear directly. Take a deep breath, you can do this. Remember the skills you have learned (e.g., deep breathing, positive self-talk, and visualization).

1. Review the hierarchy of situations and experiences from least to most anxiety provoking that you constructed in the exercise "Facing Fears—Part I."
2. Break each level down into steps like before. Make a chart like the one that follows to help you.

| Level 1 | Be able to walk around the block. |
|---|---|
| Step 1 | Open door and look outside for five minutes. |
| Step 2 | Walk out to the curb. |
| Step 3 | Walk to the corner. |
| Step 4 | Walk halfway around the block. |
| Step 5 | Walk all the way around the block. |

| Level 1 | |
|---|---|
| Step 1 | |
| Step 2 | |
| Step 3 | |
| Step 4 | |
| Step 5 | |

Exercise II.D

3. Remember to use the coping skills of deep breathing, visualization, and positive self-talk.
4. Continue to face each fear until your rating of this situation decreases to zero or no higher than three.
5. Journal about your attempts each day and discuss in your next group session.

# Section III

# ANGER CONTROL PROBLEMS

Therapist's Overview

# ANGER LOG

## GOALS OF THE EXERCISE

1. Identify the physiological, cognitive, and behavioral signs of anger.
2. Get a sense of how often you become angry.
3. Get a sense of what situations trigger feelings of anger.
4. Begin to develop a sense of how others perceive your anger.

## ADDITIONAL HOMEWORK THAT MAY BE APPLICABLE TO ANGER

- Assertiveness Deficit         Is It Passive, Aggressive, or Assertive?   Page 46
- Domestic Violence Offenders   When Do I Need a Break?                     Page 133

## ADDITIONAL PROBLEMS IN WHICH THIS EXERCISE MAY BE USEFUL

- Anxiety

## SUGGESTIONS FOR PROCESSING THIS EXERCISE WITH THE CLIENT

When people become angry, it is important for them to become aware of their bodily reactions, thought patterns, and actual behaviors. By increasing their awareness of these factors, group members can begin to take control and reduce them. The following exercise will help group members keep track of what triggers their anger, as well as what they think about and do when they become angry.

Exercise III.A

# ANGER LOG

For you to change what happens when you become angry, you first need to get in tune with your bodily reactions and thoughts, as well as what you actually do when you become angry. Once you get a handle on these three factors, how you want to change can then be planned. The following exercise will help guide you through what happens when you become angry.

1. During the next week or so, think about the times you become angry, and answer the following questions with a *yes* or *no*.

   When I was angry, I noticed that my heart was pounding harder, faster, or louder.
   _____
   _____

   When I was angry, I noticed that my muscles felt tense or tight.
   _____
   _____

   This was especially true for my (indicate the part of your body).
   _____
   _____

   When I was angry, I noticed that my skin felt hotter or became red.
   _____
   _____

   When I was angry, I could feel the adrenaline rushing through my body.
   _____
   _____

   Describe any other physiological reaction when you were angry.
   _____
   _____

Exercise III.A

2. Use the following charts to log the times that you become angry.

| Date | Time | Situation (describe what was going on) |
|------|------|----------------------------------------|
|      |      |                                        |
|      |      |                                        |
|      |      |                                        |
|      |      |                                        |
|      |      |                                        |
|      |      |                                        |

| Rating of anger | Anger-triggering thoughts (describe what was going through your mind) | Angry behavior (describe what you did) |
|-----------------|----------------------------------------------------------------------|----------------------------------------|
|                 |                                                                      |                                        |
|                 |                                                                      |                                        |
|                 |                                                                      |                                        |
|                 |                                                                      |                                        |
|                 |                                                                      |                                        |
|                 |                                                                      |                                        |

Therapist's Overview

# IS IT ANGER OR AGGRESSION?

## GOALS OF THE EXERCISE

1. Identify your anger cycle.
2. Develop an understanding of the difference between feeling angry and acting aggressively.

## ADDITIONAL HOMEWORK THAT MAY BE APPLICABLE TO ANGER

- Assertiveness Deficit          Is It Passive, Aggressive, or Assertive?     Page 46
- Domestic Violence Offenders    When Do I Need a Break?                      Page 133

## ADDITIONAL PROBLEMS IN WHICH THIS EXERCISE MAY BE USEFUL

- Anxiety

## SUGGESTIONS FOR PROCESSING THIS EXERCISE WITH THE CLIENT

A key issue in helping individuals to control their anger is helping them to understand the difference between feeling angry and acting aggressive. Many individuals who are confronted about their anger misperceive or misunderstand that the problem is not that they feel angry, but that they are aggressive. It is important to explain that all feelings, including anger, are okay. However, how we express our feelings needs to be appropriate. This exercise is designed to help individuals get a clearer understanding of how to appropriately express anger. Individuals will need to complete the previous homework (Exercise III.A, "Anger Log") in order to complete this assignment. Before giving this homework, be sure to explain that anger is an emotion or feeling, and aggression is a behavior.

Exercise III.B

# IS IT ANGER OR AGGRESSION?

All of us experience feelings of anger; however, we don't all express anger the same way. A common problem is deciphering our angry feelings from our angry behavior. Although feelings are neither right nor wrong, behaviors certainly are. The following exercise will help you develop a clearer sense of whether you express your angry feelings or behave aggressively. Review your anger log to complete the following.

1. Anger results from being or feeling hurt. This can be physical and/or emotional hurt. In reviewing your anger log, complete the following sentence for each time that you became angry.

    When I became angry, I felt hurt because _____.

    When I became angry, I felt hurt because _____.

    When I became angry, I felt hurt because _____.

    When I became angry, I felt hurt because _____.

    When I became angry, I felt hurt because _____.

    When I became angry, I felt hurt because _____.

    When I became angry, I felt hurt because _____.

    When I became angry, I felt hurt because _____.

    When I became angry, I felt hurt because _____.

Exercise III.B

When I became angry, I felt hurt because _____
_____.

2. Review your anger log and what you did (your behavior) each time you became angry. Answer the following for each time you became angry and describe why it was or was not aggressive behavior.

When I became angry I (describe your behavior after becoming angry) _____
_____.

This was aggressive behavior because _____
_____.

This was not aggressive behavior because _____
_____.

When I became angry I (describe your behavior after becoming angry) _____
_____.

This was aggressive behavior because _____
_____.

This was not aggressive behavior because _____
_____.

When I became angry I (describe your behavior after becoming angry) _____
_____.

This was aggressive behavior because _____
_____.

This was not aggressive behavior because _____
_____.

When I became angry I (describe your behavior after becoming angry) _____
_____.

This was aggressive behavior because _____
_____.

This was not aggressive behavior because _____
_____.

When I became angry I (describe your behavior after becoming angry) _____
_____.

This was aggressive behavior because _____
_____.

Exercise III.B

This was not aggressive behavior because _____
_____.

    When I became angry I (describe your behavior after becoming angry) _____
_____.

This was aggressive behavior because _____
_____.

This was not aggressive behavior because _____
_____.

    When I became angry I (describe your behavior after becoming angry) _____
_____.

This was aggressive behavior because _____
_____.

This was not aggressive behavior because _____
_____.

    When I became angry I (describe your behavior after becoming angry) _____
_____.

This was aggressive behavior because _____
_____.

This was not aggressive behavior because _____
_____.

    When I became angry I (describe your behavior after becoming angry) _____
_____.

This was aggressive behavior because _____
_____.

This was not aggressive behavior because _____
_____.

    When I became angry I (describe your behavior after becoming angry) _____
_____.

This was aggressive behavior because _____
_____.

This was not aggressive behavior because _____
_____.

Review this assignment with your group.

Therapist's Overview

# GO BLOW OUT SOME CANDLES*

## GOALS OF THE EXERCISE

1. Begin to develop control over your anger.
2. Learn a way to relax more.

## ADDITIONAL HOMEWORK THAT MAY BE APPLICABLE TO ANGER

- Assertiveness Deficit          Is It Passive, Aggressive, or Assertive?   Page 46
- Domestic Violence Offenders    When Do I Need a Break?                    Page 133
- Domestic Violence Survivors    What If . . . ?                            Page 144
- Type-A Stress                  Where's My Tension?                        Page 263

## ADDITIONAL PROBLEMS IN WHICH THIS EXERCISE MAY BE USEFUL

- Anxiety

## SUGGESTIONS FOR PROCESSING THIS EXERCISE WITH THE CLIENT

Because anger can be physically dangerous and can lead to problems in many areas of one's life, it is important for individuals to learn how to redirect and reduce such feelings. Once individuals have learned some of the triggers to their anger and the physiological, cognitive, and behavioral responses to anger, it is important for them to learn how to redirect and prevent themselves from losing control.

---

*This exercise was first described by Bevilacqua, L., & Dattilio, F. (2001) *Brief Family Therapy Homework Planner.* New York: John Wiley & Sons.

Exercise III.C

# GO BLOW OUT SOME CANDLES

**PRACTICE THE EXERCISE AT LEAST ONCE A DAY FOR THE NEXT WEEK**

When feeling the initial signs of anger, practice taking a deep breath. To do so, breathe in through your nose. When you do, picture a balloon in your belly that you are trying to blow up. As you exhale through your mouth, count to three. You can also picture blowing out a candle. Try to blow up 8 to 10 balloons and blow out 8 to 10 candles. If you are still feeling angry and tense after the 10th balloon or candle, practice doing deep muscle relaxation for every muscle group in your body.

Report back to your group on your success in using this relaxation and visualization technique.

Therapist's Overview

# MY SAFE PLACE*

## GOALS OF THE EXERCISE

1. Develop a sense of security and comfort no matter where you are or what time it is.
2. Be able to focus and reassure yourself that you are okay.
3. Be able to access that safe place whenever you feel frightened or insecure.

## ADDITIONAL HOMEWORK THAT MAY BE APPLICABLE TO ANGER CONTROL PROBLEMS

- Agoraphobia/Panic           Facing Fears—Part One                       Page 17
- Assertiveness Deficit       Is It Passive, Aggressive, or Assertive?    Page 46
- Domestic Violence Offenders When Do I Need a Break?                     Page 133

## ADDITIONAL PROBLEMS IN WHICH THIS EXERCISE MAY BE USEFUL

- Anxiety
- Depression

## SUGGESTIONS FOR PROCESSING THIS EXERCISE WITH THE CLIENT

When people feel overly angry, they can also feel out of control. To help reduce such feelings, which tend to be circular and self-reinforcing, have them discover a safe place. This safe place will be theirs alone. They can go there anytime they want as often as they like or need. Explain to them that through the use of imagery and visualization, a person can ideally access their safe place anytime, day or night, no matter where they are or whom they are with. This safe place can be a literal or figurative place and represents a place where a person feels protected and able to truly relax without worrying. The following exercise provides a pathway to creating a safe place. Before this task can be assigned, be sure to review deep breathing and basic relaxation skills.

---

*This exercise was first described by Bevilacqua, L., & Dattilio, F. (2001) *Brief Family Therapy Homework Planner.* New York: John Wiley & Sons.

Exercise III.D

# MY SAFE PLACE

Creating a safe place is ideal anytime you want to escape feeling tense, irritable, anxious, angry, and so forth. It can be a literal place that you have been to or a figurative place that you can imagine. This safe place is yours alone and you have control over when you go there and how long you stay.

Once you have identified a safe place, describe and record as many details as you can.

My special safe place is _____
_____.

Describe your safe place. (What does it look like? What does it smell like? How big is it? What is in your safe place? What color is it?)
_____
_____
_____
_____.

I feel safe there because _____
_____
_____.

When I visit my safe place I feel _____ because _____
_____
_____.

Practice visualizing and experiencing your safe place at least once a day over the next week and whenever you feel stressed. Report your experiences in the next group meeting.

# Section IV

# ANXIETY

Therapist's Overview

# WHAT HAPPENS WHEN I FEEL ANXIOUS?

## GOALS OF THE EXERCISE

1. Externalize feelings of anxiety by recording the contributing factors to being anxious.
2. Be able to identify negative/anxious self-talk.
3. Be able to identify negative/anxious behavior.

## ADDITIONAL HOMEWORK THAT MAY BE APPLICABLE TO ANXIETY

- Agoraphobia/Panic         Breaking My Panic Cycle         Page 14
- Agoraphobia/Panic         Facing Fears—Part One          Page 17

## ADDITIONAL PROBLEMS IN WHICH THIS EXERCISE MAY BE USEFUL

- Anger Control Problems
- Depression

## SUGGESTIONS FOR PROCESSING THIS EXERCISE WITH THE CLIENT

Anxiety can become a debilitating life experience. Individuals need to understand what happens when they are feeling anxious from a physiological, cognitive, and behavioral viewpoint. In group, review the physiological signs such as shortness of breath, increased heart and/or pulse rate, dizziness, nausea, shakiness, and so forth. Group members should be aware of such symptoms and when they are experiencing them. If they are such, the following exercise will help them identify typical triggers to anxiety as well as their accompanying thoughts and behaviors.

Exercise IV.A

# WHAT HAPPENS WHEN I FEEL ANXIOUS?

This exercise will help you to recognize the triggers when you feel anxious, as well as your typical thoughts and behaviors. Complete each chart and rate your level of anxiety (0 represents no anxiety, and 10 represents extreme and unbearable anxiety). Once you have completed this exercise, you will be on your way to creating a game plan of how to reduce and conquer your anxiety. Over the next week, use the following chart to record each time that you feel anxious.

| Date/time | Describe the situation | Rate anxiety (0 to 10) |
|---|---|---|
|  |  |  |
|  |  |  |
|  |  |  |
|  |  |  |
|  |  |  |

When a person has a problem with anxiety, it is very common for him/her to think the worst (e.g., I'll never be able to overcome this). It is also common for him/her to react by withdrawing and isolating (e.g., staying home and not going out with friends) or by engaging in activities that are not healthy (e.g., drinking or smoking).

For each of the previous situations described, complete the following two charts.

Describe what was going through your mind when you felt anxious.

_____
_____
_____
_____
_____
_____
_____
_____

Exercise IV.A

Describe what you did when you felt anxious.

Therapist's Overview

# WHAT ELSE CAN I SAY OR DO?

## GOALS OF THE EXERCISE

1. Be able to change negative/anxious self-talk to more self-adaptive and positive self-talk.
2. Be able to change negative/anxious behavior to more self-adaptive and positive behavior.

## ADDITIONAL HOMEWORK THAT MAY BE APPLICABLE TO ANXIETY

- Agoraphobia/Panic    Breaking My Panic Cycle    Page 14
- Agoraphobia/Panic    Facing Fears—Part One    Page 17

## ADDITIONAL PROBLEMS IN WHICH THIS EXERCISE MAY BE USEFUL

- Agoraphobia/Panic
- Anger Control Problems
- Bulimia
- Depression
- Phobias—Specific/Social

## SUGGESTIONS FOR PROCESSING THIS EXERCISE WITH THE CLIENT

This exercise is to follow the exercise "When Is This Going to Happen?" (see Section II). Review that exercise with the group, and brainstorm a list of alternative thoughts and behaviors that each person can rely on when they feel anxious. Have group members complete the chart in this exercise and use it throughout the week whenever they feel anxious. When they use it, instruct them to rate the effectiveness of each alternative thought and/or behavior they try.

Exercise IV.B

# WHAT ELSE CAN I SAY OR DO?

During your session, you should use the first chart to identify a list of alternative thoughts, which you can try out the next time you feel anxious. After each one that you try, rate how effective you felt it to be on a scale of 0 (representing no anxiety) to 10 (representing uncontrollable and overwhelming anxiety). Repeat this same process as it applies to anxious behaviors.

List of alternative thoughts to say to myself:

1. _____
2. _____
3. _____
4. _____
5. _____
6. _____
7. _____
8. _____
9. _____
10. _____

Use the following chart to record the thoughts that go through your mind when feeling anxious and a rating of how anxious you feel. Also, record an alternative thought that is more adaptive and positive, and rate your level of anxiety again.

| These were my negative/anxious thoughts. | Rating (0 to 10) | This is what I will say to myself instead. | Rating (0 to 10) |
|---|---|---|---|
| | | | |
| | | | |
| | | | |
| | | | |
| | | | |

Exercise IV.B

List of alternative behaviors that I can do when feeling anxious:
1. _____
2. _____
3. _____
4. _____
5. _____
6. _____
7. _____
8. _____
9. _____
10. _____

Use the following chart to record the behaviors in which you engage when feeling anxious and a rating of how anxious you feel. Also, record an alternative behavior, which is more adaptive and positive, and rate your level of anxiety again.

| These are the negative/anxious behaviors I usually do (or did). | Rating (0 to 10) | This is what I will do instead. | Rating (0 to 10) |
|---|---|---|---|
| | | | |
| | | | |
| | | | |
| | | | |
| | | | |

These charts can be used whenever you are feeling anxious and want to regain control of your life. In your next group meeting, discuss your experiences in trying the alternative thoughts and behaviors.

Therapist's Overview

# BEATING SELF-DEFEATING BELIEFS

## GOALS OF THE EXERCISE

1. Identify when self-defeating beliefs are interfering and fueling anxiety-provoking thinking.
2. Learn ways to challenge self-defeating beliefs, and replace them with positive self-affirmations.

## ADDITIONAL HOMEWORK THAT MAY BE APPLICABLE TO ANXIETY

- Agoraphobia/Panic  Breaking My Panic Cycle  Page 14
- Agoraphobia/Panic  Facing Fears—Part One  Page 17
- Depression  Taking Charge of Your Thoughts  Page 126

## ADDITIONAL PROBLEMS IN WHICH THIS EXERCISE MAY BE USEFUL

- Anger Control Problems
- Bulimia
- Codependency
- Depression

## SUGGESTIONS FOR PROCESSING THIS EXERCISE WITH THE CLIENT

Individuals dealing with anxiety are often faced with negative and self-defeating beliefs (e.g., "If people see who I really am, they won't be my friend/won't like me," or "I don't deserve to be happy," or "I could never travel by plane, it's not safe"). These beliefs often lead to and fuel other anxiety-provoking cognitions (e.g., "Things will never get any better"). It would be helpful for group members to review and make a list of the common cognitive distortions in which they engage. Individuals also need to learn how these beliefs and thoughts prevent them from living satisfying and healthy lives. The following exercise is designed to help them challenge such distorted thinking and beliefs by replacing them with positive self-affirming thoughts.

**Exercise IV.C**

# BEATING SELF-DEFEATING BELIEFS

This exercise is designed to help you challenge the negative types of thoughts and beliefs you have that fuel feelings of anxiety. After you have reviewed and made a list of the various types of negative and self-defeating beliefs you think about, complete the following exercise to learn how to challenge and beat them.

Over the next week or so, record times you catch yourself thinking about your negative and self-defeating beliefs. Use the following chart to describe the situation in which you were thinking this way. Record the belief and rate the level to which you agree and believe in that particular thought or belief. A rating of 0 represents that you do not believe in that belief at all, and a rating of 10 represents that you totally and completely agree with and believe in that belief.

| Describe the situation | Record your self-defeating belief | Rating |
|---|---|---|
| | | |
| | | |
| | | |
| | | |
| | | |
| | | |
| | | |
| | | |
| | | |
| | | |

Use the following chart to practice replacing the negative self-defeating belief or cognition with a self-affirming statement. Once you have recorded this more positive and self-adaptive statement, rate your belief in it. A rating of 0 represents no belief in that statement, and a rating of 10 represents 100 percent agreement and belief in that statement.

Exercise IV.C

| Positive self-affirming statement | Rating |
|---|---|
|  |  |
|  |  |
|  |  |
|  |  |
|  |  |
|  |  |
|  |  |
|  |  |
|  |  |
|  |  |

The more you practice this exercise, you should notice greater and greater agreement in the positive self-affirming statements and less belief in the negative self-defeating beliefs. Share your experiences and struggles in doing this exercise with the other group members.

## Section V

# ASSERTIVENESS DEFICIT

Therapist's Overview

# IS IT PASSIVE, AGGRESSIVE, OR ASSERTIVE?

## GOALS OF THE EXERCISE

1. Develop a clearer understanding of what it means to be assertive, passive, and aggressive.
2. Be able to cite examples that depict assertive, passive, and aggressive behaviors.

## ADDITIONAL HOMEWORK THAT MAY BE APPLICABLE TO ASSERTIVENESS DEFICIT

- Anxiety              Beating Self-Defeating Beliefs      Page 42
- Codependence         I Feel . . .                        Page 117
- Shyness              What Comes after Hi?                Page 242

## ADDITIONAL PROBLEMS IN WHICH THIS EXERCISE MAY BE USEFUL

- Anger Control Problems
- Codependency

## SUGGESTIONS FOR PROCESSING THIS EXERCISE WITH THE CLIENT

Individuals who lack assertiveness will respond to situations either passively or aggressively. Usually, aggressive behavior occurs after being passive for a long while and then no longer being able to "take it." Individuals who lack assertiveness need to understand not only what it means to be assertive but also what it means to be passive or aggressive. In a group session, process the differences of each behavior by defining and acting it out (e.g., role-play or model). Once each member has a clear understanding of the differences, suggest the following exercise, which will help them to recognize these behaviors in their daily life.

Exercise V.A

# IS IT PASSIVE, AGGRESSIVE, OR ASSERTIVE?

For you to develop assertiveness, it is important to understand not only what it means to be assertive but also what it means to be passive or aggressive. After you have discussed such differences in treatment, complete the following exercise.

Define each of the following:

To be passive means to _____

_____

An example of someone being passive is _____

_____

To be aggressive means to _____

_____

An example of someone being aggressive is _____

_____

To be assertive means to _____

_____

An example of someone being assertive is _____

_____.

Over the next week, use the following format to track your behavior. Record the date and describe the situation surrounding your behavior first, and then describe how you responded or acted. Tell whether you were passive, aggressive, or assertive and why you think so. If you did not respond in an assertive manner, describe why and how you could next time.

Exercise V.A

Date: _____
Situation: _____
_____
_____.

What I did in this situation: _____
_____
_____.

This was_____ because_____
_____.

If this was not an assertive response, describe what prevented you from being assertive (e.g., thoughts, fears such as "he or she would get mad at me," or, "he or she would not like me," or, "it wouldn't have made a difference"). _____
_____.

Describe how you could have responded in an assertive manner if you did not have those negative thoughts or fears. _____
_____
_____
_____.


Date: _____
Situation: _____
_____
_____.

What I did in this situation: _____
_____
_____.

This was_____ because_____
_____.

If this was not an assertive response, describe what prevented you from being assertive (e.g., thoughts, fears such as "he or she would get mad at me," or, "he or she would not like me," or, "it wouldn't have made a difference"). _____
_____.

Describe how you could have responded in an assertive manner if you did not have those negative thoughts or fears. _____
_____
_____.

Exercise V.A

Date: _____

Situation: _____

_____

_____.

What I did in this situation: _____

_____

_____.

This was _____ because _____

_____

_____.

If this was not an assertive response, describe what prevented you from being assertive (e.g., thoughts, fears such as "he or she would get mad at me," or, "he or she would not like me," or, "it wouldn't have made a difference"). _____

_____.

Describe how you could have responded in an assertive manner if you did not have those negative thoughts or fears. _____

_____

_____

_____.

Date: _____

Situation: _____

_____

_____.

What I did in this situation: _____

_____

_____.

This was _____ because _____

_____

_____.

If this was not an assertive response, describe what prevented you from being assertive (e.g., thoughts, fears such as "he or she would get mad at me," or, "he or she would not like me," or, "it wouldn't have made a difference"). _____

_____.

Describe how you could have responded in an assertive manner if you did not have those negative thoughts or fears. _____

_____

_____

_____.

Exercise V.A

Date: _____

Situation: _____
_____
_____.

What I did in this situation: _____
_____
_____.

This was_____ because_____
_____
_____.

If this was not an assertive response, describe what prevented you from being assertive (e.g., thoughts, fears such as "he or she would get mad at me," or, "he or she would not like me," or, "it wouldn't have made a difference"). _____
_____.

Describe how you could have responded in an assertive manner if you did not have those negative thoughts or fears. _____
_____
_____
_____.

Date: _____

Situation: _____
_____
_____.

What I did in this situation: _____
_____
_____.

This was_____ because_____
_____
_____.

If this was not an assertive response, describe what prevented you from being assertive (e.g., thoughts, fears such as "he or she would get mad at me," or, "he or she would not like me," or, "it wouldn't have made a difference"). _____
_____.

Describe how you could have responded in an assertive manner if you did not have those negative thoughts or fears. _____
_____
_____
_____.

Review this with your group.

Therapist's Overview

# IT'S OKAY TO BE ASSERTIVE

## GOALS OF THE EXERCISE

1. Identify the fears that individuals have when it comes to being assertive.
2. Learn ways that individuals can overcome their fears of being assertive.

## ADDITIONAL HOMEWORK THAT MAY BE APPLICABLE TO ASSERTIVENESS DEFICIT

| | | |
|---|---|---|
| • Anxiety | Beating Self-Defeating Thoughts | Page 42 |
| • Codependence | I Feel . . . | Page 117 |
| • Shyness | What Comes after Hi? | Page 242 |

## ADDITIONAL PROBLEMS IN WHICH THIS EXERCISE MAY BE USEFUL

- Codependence
- Shyness
- Vocational Stress

## SUGGESTIONS FOR PROCESSING THIS EXERCISE WITH THE CLIENT

This exercise is designed to help individuals begin to recognize what prevents them from being assertive, as well as what they can do about it. In a group session, review some of the common reasons given by individuals to not be assertive (e.g., fear of failure or fear of rejection). Help individuals to identify a list of self-talk statements, which can challenge such fears. Have them also construct a list of responses and/or techniques to demonstrate assertiveness (e.g., broken-record, acknowledgment technique, clouding, slowing the conversation down). Have them discuss and record a description of each type of assertiveness response. Once they have these lists, have them complete the following exercise.

Exercise V.B

# IT'S OKAY TO BE ASSERTIVE

This exercise will help you to challenge the obstacles that keep you from being assertive. Be sure to review your lists of positive self-talk statements and assertiveness responses on a daily basis. Some assertiveness response are as follows:

- *Broken-record response.* A short, clear statement that you repeat continually (e.g., "I need to leave now.").
- *Acknowledgment response.* You recognize and acknowledge accurate and constructive feedback (e.g., "You're right, I forgot to bring home some milk.").
- *Slowing-the-conversation-down response.* This helps you to reduce the pressure of feeling like you have to react (e.g., "That's important and I want to understand what you mean, could you say that again?).

Try a positive self-talk statement and an assertiveness response at least three times over the next week. Use the following format to track situations in which you practiced being assertive and which self-talk statements and assertiveness response you tried. Afterward, rate how effective this was for you.

Describe a situation in which you responded assertively.

_____
_____
_____

What self-talk statement did you use?

_____
_____

Describe your assertive response.

_____

Rate how effective you felt this technique to be.
____ Not effective   ____ Somewhat effective   ____ Very effective   ____ Excellent

Describe a situation in which you responded assertively.

_____
_____
_____

Exercise V.B

What self-talk statement did you use?
_____

Describe your assertive response.
_____

Rate how effective you felt this technique to be.
____ Not effective    ____ Somewhat effective    ____ Very effective    ____ Excellent

Describe a situation in which you responded assertively.
_____
_____
_____

What self-talk statement did you use?
_____

Describe your assertive response.
_____

Rate how effective you felt this technique to be.
____ Not effective    ____ Somewhat effective    ____ Very effective    ____ Excellent

Describe a situation in which you responded assertively.
_____
_____
_____

What self-talk statement did you use?
_____

Describe your assertive response.
_____

Rate how effective you felt this technique to be.
____ Not effective    ____ Somewhat effective    ____ Very effective    ____ Excellent

Share your experience with the group.

# Section VI

# BULIMIA

Therapist's Overview

# AM I HUNGRY?

## GOALS OF THE EXERCISE

1. Recognize when you are feeling physical hunger, and distinguish that from emotional hunger.
2. Identify and begin to acknowledge your own feelings, which are triggers to emotional hunger.

## ADDITIONAL HOMEWORK THAT MAY BE APPLICABLE TO BULIMIA

- Anger Control Problems    My Safe Place    Page 33
- Anxiety    Beating Self-Defeating Beliefs    Page 42
- Codependence    I Feel . . .    Page 117
- Depression    Taking Charge of Your Thoughts    Page 126

## ADDITIONAL PROBLEMS IN WHICH THIS EXERCISE MAY BE USEFUL

- Anger Control Problems
- Anxiety
- Depression

## SUGGESTIONS FOR PROCESSING THIS EXERCISE WITH THE CLIENT

Most individuals with an eating disorder do not clearly understand the difference between eating because of feeling physically hungry and eating because of emotional needs that are not being expressed or met. For individuals to get control of their eating behavior, they must learn to recognize when they are feeling physically hungry and need to eat, as opposed to eating because of emotional stress. Before assigning this task, have group members refer to their eating journals or think about times they ate today. Ask them to describe how they were feeling when they ate and if they *felt* hungry. Have them describe what a hunger pain feels like. Let them know that the following assignment will help them to tune in to their body sensations and to recognize when they are actually experiencing physical hunger versus an emotional need to eat.

Exercise VI.A

# AM I HUNGRY?

Many of us eat because we want to and not because we are hungry. Sometimes we may look at the clock and say, "It's dinner time," and therefore think that we should eat. Sometimes we think about stress in our life or think of how bored we are and just start eating. For us to take control of our eating behavior, we must learn to recognize when we need to eat because we are hungry versus when we eat because of some emotional need. The following exercise is designed to help you distinguish between the two. It will help you to track the frequency of your eating, how you knew you were hungry, your hunger level (1 meaning not very hungry at all and 5 meaning that you were starving), and the thoughts and feelings you had before you ate as well as afterward.

Date: _____ Time: _____ Hunger level (1 to 5): _____

Physical feelings/signs that I was hungry (e.g., stomach growling, headache, etc.): _____.

Thoughts before eating: _____.

Feelings (e.g., "I was stressed/worried/frustrated about work/my relationship/my family life"): _____.

Describe what you ate: _____.

After I ate I felt _____.

After I ate I was thinking _____.

Exercise VI.A

Date: _____ Time: _____ Hunger level (1 to 5): _____

Physical feelings/signs that I was hungry (e.g., stomach growling, headache, etc.): ___
_____
_____.

Thoughts before eating: _____
_____.

Feelings (e.g., "I was stressed/worried/frustrated about work/my relationship/my family life"):
_____
_____.

Describe what you ate: _____
_____.

After I ate I felt _____.

After I ate I was thinking _____
_____.

Date: _____ Time: _____ Hunger level (1 to 5): _____

Physical feelings/signs that I was hungry (e.g., stomach growling, headache, etc.): ___
_____
_____.

Thoughts before eating: _____
_____.

Feelings (e.g., "I was stressed/worried/frustrated about work/my relationship/my family life"):
_____
_____.

Describe what you ate: _____
_____.

After I ate I felt _____.

After I ate I was thinking _____
_____.

**Exercise VI.A**

Date: _____ Time: _____ Hunger level (1 to 5): _____

Physical feelings/signs that I was hungry (e.g., stomach growling, headache, etc.): ___
_____
_____.

Thoughts before eating:
_____.

Feelings (e.g., "I was stressed/worried/frustrated about work/my relationship/my family life"):
_____
_____.

Describe what you ate:
_____.

After I ate I felt _____.

After I ate I was thinking _____
_____.

Therapist's Overview

# I NEED TO GET CONTROL*

## GOALS OF THE EXERCISE

1. Gain some control over the frequency of eating, dieting, and weight controlling behaviors.
2. Get a sense of how often these behaviors are occurring.

## ADDITIONAL HOMEWORK THAT MAY BE APPLICABLE TO BULIMIA

- Anger Control Problems        My Safe Place                       Page 33
- Anxiety                       Beating Self-Defeating Beliefs      Page 42
- Codependence                  I Feel . . .                        Page 117
- Depression                    Taking Charge of Your Thoughts      Page 126

## ADDITIONAL PROBLEMS IN WHICH THIS EXERCISE MAY BE USEFUL

- Agoraphobia/Panic
- Anger Control Problems

## SUGGESTIONS FOR PROCESSING THIS EXERCISE WITH THE CLIENT

Some of the most effective treatment interventions for treating an individual with bulimia or any other type of eating disorder have relied on the use of linking one's thoughts and behaviors. As a result, the following exercise utilizes this cognitive-behavioral approach to help individuals get a handle and some control over their thoughts and behaviors regarding eating.

---

*This exercise was first described by Bevilacqua, L., & Dattilio, F. (2001) *Brief Family Therapy Homework Planner.* New York: John Wiley & Sons.

Exercise VI.B

# I NEED TO GET CONTROL

This exercise is designed to help you get a better sense of what goes through your mind as well as your behavior when you eat. Sometimes, our eating habits feel out of control, which makes us feel and sometimes act out of control. By tracking your thoughts and feelings, you will be able to see if there are any patterns regarding your eating. If any patterns are identified, then the changes that need to occur can be understood with greater clarity.

1. Use the following chart to identify your behavior. This refers to when you eat (e.g., "I ate lunch," or "I skipped breakfast"). It also refers to what you do after eating (e.g., "I exercised," or "I vomited").
2. Describe how you are feeling before, during, and after eating.
3. Describe what you are thinking before, during, and after eating.
4. Record the day and time.

| Behavior | | Thought | Feeling | Day | Time |
|---|---|---|---|---|---|
| | Before | | | | |
| | During | | | | |
| | After | | | | |

| Behavior | | Thought | Feeling | Day | Time |
|---|---|---|---|---|---|
| | Before | | | | |
| | During | | | | |
| | After | | | | |

| Behavior | | Thought | Feeling | Day | Time |
|---|---|---|---|---|---|
| | Before | | | | |
| | During | | | | |
| | After | | | | |

Exercise VI.B

| Behavior | | Thought | Feeling | Day | Time |
|---|---|---|---|---|---|
| | Before | | | | |
| | During | | | | |
| | After | | | | |

| Behavior | | Thought | Feeling | Day | Time |
|---|---|---|---|---|---|
| | Before | | | | |
| | During | | | | |
| | After | | | | |

**Therapist's Overview**

# WHAT AM I THINKING?

## GOALS OF THE EXERCISE

1. Identify the types of thinking errors in which the individual engages.
2. Identify the feeling you have when you think such thoughts.
3. Generate more adaptive and/or realistic self-talk, and identify alternative responses.
4. Describe the feeling that you have when you think about the alternative statement.

## ADDITIONAL HOMEWORK THAT MAY BE APPLICABLE TO BULIMIA

| | | |
|---|---|---|
| • Anger Control Problems | My Safe Place | Page 33 |
| • Anxiety | Beating Self-Defeating Beliefs | Page 42 |
| • Codependence | I Feel . . . | Page 117 |
| • Depression | Taking Charge of Your Thoughts | Page 126 |

## ADDITIONAL PROBLEMS IN WHICH THIS EXERCISE MAY BE USEFUL

- Agoraphobia/Panic
- Anger Control Problems
- Anxiety
- Chemical Dependence
- Depression

## SUGGESTIONS FOR PROCESSING THIS EXERCISE WITH THE CLIENT

Individuals with an eating disorder are thinking constantly in their heads and engage in various types of cognitive distortions. They may think that if they start eating they won't be able to stop. They may believe that the only way to look good is to exercise and not eat. Such thoughts are generally based in some kind of fear (i.e., becoming overweight, losing control, being rejected, etc.). It is important for these individuals to get such thoughts and fears out of their head and to externalize them. Review the list of cognitive distortions with the group and be sure that each person has a good understanding of each type of distortion. Be sure to use plenty of examples.

Exercise VI.C

# WHAT AM I THINKING?

Sometimes you may think that if you start eating you won't be able to stop. You may believe that the only way to look good is to exercise and not eat. Such thoughts are generally based in some kind of fear (i.e., becoming overweight, losing control, being rejected, etc.). It is important for you to externalize such thoughts and fears. This exercise is designed to help you begin the process of overcoming and letting go of such powerful and overwhelming thinking.

1. Review the following list of common cognitive distortions.
   - *Arbitrary inference.* Making conclusions in the absence of substantiating evidence (e.g., "If I am not a perfect body weight, no one will like me").
   - *Catastrophizing.* Thinking about consequences and blowing them out of proportion in a negative way. For example, you are counting points for a Weight Watchers program or calories for the day and you go over your allotted number. You respond by saying, "I can't believe I did that. I might as well give up now because I can never stick to anything."
   - *Dark glasses, or mental filtering.* Blocking out the positives and just focusing on the negatives. For example, two of your friends meet you at the mall. One friend remarks about how good you look. You begin to think that your other friend must believe that you look pretty awful.
   - *Dichotomous thinking, or black-and-white thinking.* Codifying experiences as either all or nothing (e.g., "I am either fat or not—there's no in-between").
   - *Discounting.* Rejecting the positive things that happen to you. For example, over a week's time, you refrain from purging for four days. Instead of looking at the positive, you think, "I am so weak, I purged on three days this past week."
   - *Mind reading.* Assuming what others are thinking without the benefit of verbal communication (e.g., "I know that when people look at me, they think that I am too fat").
   - *Tunnel vision.* Seeing what fits one's current state of mind (e.g., "If I eat only foods with starch, I'll get fat and won't be able to lose the weight").

2. Use the chart to record the various thinking errors in which you engage over the next week.

3. Record the type of distortion and the feeling you experience.

| Thought | Type of distortion | Feeling |
|---------|-------------------|---------|
|  |  |  |
|  |  |  |
|  |  |  |
|  |  |  |
|  |  |  |

4. Record an alternative and more adaptive and positive statement, which you could use in the future. Also record the feeling you have when you change your thinking.

| Alternative thought | Feeling |
|--------------------|---------|
|  |  |
|  |  |
|  |  |
|  |  |
|  |  |

Therapist's Overview

# IS IT GOOD FOOD OR BAD FOOD? SHOULD IT MATTER THAT MUCH?

## GOALS OF THE EXERCISE

1. Be able to challenge the "good food" versus "bad food" distorted thinking, and begin to allow oneself the freedom to eat the bad food without feeling guilty or needing to purge.
2. Identify ways to prevent purging after eating bad food.

## ADDITIONAL HOMEWORK THAT MAY BE APPLICABLE TO BULIMIA

- Anger Control Problems  My Safe Place  Page 33
- Anxiety  Beating Self-Defeating Beliefs  Page 42
- Assertiveness Deficit  It's Okay to Be Assertive  Page 51
- Codependence  I Feel . . .  Page 117
- Depression  Taking Charge of Your Thoughts  Page 126

## ADDITIONAL PROBLEMS IN WHICH THIS EXERCISE MAY BE USEFUL

- Anxiety (Substitute foods for behavior in which you engage that increases or decreases anxiety.)
- Depression (Substitute foods for behavior in which you engage that increases or decreases depression.)

## SUGGESTIONS FOR PROCESSING THIS EXERCISE WITH THE CLIENT

Individuals who suffer with bulimia, as well as those who are very concerned about their eating, often categorize food as *good* or *bad*. When they eat a bad food, they frequently feel guilty, angry, depressed, and try to reduce such negative feelings by purging. This exercise is designed to help these individuals break out of such rigid thinking and to allow themselves the flexibility and freedom to eat without feeling bad. It is also designed to help individuals redirect and overcome common trigger situations to purging. Before assigning this task, review various ways to prevent a purging episode. There are several suggestions included in the homework, which you can add to.

Exercise VI.D

# IS IT GOOD FOOD OR BAD FOOD? SHOULD IT MATTER THAT MUCH?

Those of us who are very concerned about what we eat will frequently perceive food as either *good* or *bad*. When we eat the bad food, we sometimes (or maybe always) feel bad, angry, depressed, and so on. To reduce such negative feelings about ourselves, we may purge the bad food to get rid of the bad feelings, as well as the bad food itself. The following exercise is designed to help break that negative cycle, which can feel so powerful and overwhelming.

1. List your top 10 good foods and your top 10 bad foods. Rate the 10 bad food choices, with 1 representing bad and 10 representing the worst.

| Good food | Bad food | Rating |
|-----------|----------|--------|
|           |          |        |
|           |          |        |
|           |          |        |
|           |          |        |
|           |          |        |
|           |          |        |
|           |          |        |
|           |          |        |
|           |          |        |
|           |          |        |

Exercise VI.D

2. Pick the least bad food, and eat it once this week. Record the date and time and the food you eat.

   | Date | Time | Food |
   |------|------|------|
   |      |      |      |
   |      |      |      |
   |      |      |      |
   |      |      |      |
   |      |      |      |

3. Describe your thoughts and feelings after you ate this food.

   _____
   _____
   _____.

4. Describe what you did to prevent yourself from purging. Following are several options:

   I restructured my thoughts. Describe what you said to restructure your negative thinking.

   _____
   _____.

   I used a thought-stopping technique (e.g., snapped a rubber band on my wrist, said *stop* to myself, etc.). Describe which one you used.

   _____.

   I called for support. The person whom I called was _____.

   I kept busy by doing (describe what you did) _____
   _____
   _____.

   I stayed in view of others. (Tell who was around you and knew that you were trying to prevent yourself from purging.)

   _____
   _____.

   Other. (What else if anything did you do to prevent yourself from purging?) _____
   _____
   _____.

5. Share your experience with your group members and therapist(s).

# Section VII

# CAREGIVER BURNOUT

Therapist's Overview

# BEING A CAREGIVER MAKES ME FEEL . . .

## GOALS OF THE EXERCISE

1. Identify the positive and negative effects of being a caregiver.
2. Identify the feelings that are associated with being a caregiver.

## ADDITIONAL HOMEWORK THAT MAY BE APPLICABLE TO CAREGIVER BURNOUT

- Assertiveness Deficit    It's Okay to Be Assertive          Page 51
- Type-A Stress            Where's My Tension?                Page 263
- Type-A Stress            When I Feel Tension/Stress I Can . . .  Page 266

## ADDITIONAL PROBLEMS IN WHICH THIS EXERCISE MAY BE USEFUL

- Adult Children of Alcoholics
- Codependency

## SUGGESTIONS FOR PROCESSING THIS EXERCISE WITH THE CLIENT

Being a caregiver can be an overwhelming task. Often, such individuals feel taken for granted, trapped, angry, resentful, exhausted, and so forth. At the same time, however, these same individuals feel like they cannot voice such negative feelings. For their own mental health, it is imperative that they are able to voice any and all feelings that are associated with being a caregiver. This exercise is one way for them to give voice to their feelings.

Exercise VII.A

# BEING A CAREGIVER MAKES ME FEEL . . .

Being a caregiver can be very rewarding as well as extremely demanding. Often, you may feel unable to express any negative feelings about being a caregiver. This exercise was developed to let you know that your feelings are valid and to provide you with a way to express them.

1. Because being a caregiver has its positive and negative points, take the time to list what you believe to be the benefits, as well as the difficulties, to being in this role.

| Benefit | This makes me feel |
|---|---|
| | |
| | |
| | |
| | |
| | |
| | |
| | |
| | |

| Difficulty | This makes me feel |
|---|---|
| | |
| | |
| | |
| | |
| | |
| | |
| | |
| | |

Therapist's Overview

# THIS IS FOR ME AND THAT'S OKAY

## GOALS OF THE EXERCISE

1. Take time for the caregiver to remember how important he/she is.
2. Find ways to refresh and replenish the caregiver's emotional and physical energy.

## ADDITIONAL HOMEWORK THAT MAY BE APPLICABLE TO CAREGIVER BURNOUT

- Assertiveness Deficit    It's Okay to Be Assertive    Page 51
- Type-A Stress    Where's My Tension?    Page 263
- Type-A Stress    When I Feel Tension/Stress I Can . . .    Page 266

## ADDITIONAL PROBLEMS IN WHICH THIS EXERCISE MAY BE USEFUL

- Assertiveness Deficit
- Codependence

## SUGGESTIONS FOR PROCESSING THIS EXERCISE WITH THE CLIENT

Being a caregiver can be very time-consuming. Usually the needs of the caregiver are put on hold or at the bottom of the to-do list. This exercise is intended to remind the caregiver of his/her needs and that, to be effective as a caregiver, he/she must take care of himself/herself as well. Remind him/her of how important he/she is and that his/her needs are valid and should be taken care of.

**Exercise VII.B**

# THIS IS FOR ME AND THAT'S OKAY

How many times have you put someone else's needs before your own? When do you make time for you? Being a caregiver is an admirable role, but it can also be very overwhelming. The energy you must put forth is very involved and draining. If that energy is not replenished, you will burn out and no longer be the type of caregiver you intended to be. For your own sake, as well as for the person you are taking care of, it is imperative that you take care of you, too. The following exercise will help you achieve this well-deserved reward.

1. List all of the things that you love to do (besides take care of people).

   _____
   _____
   _____
   _____
   _____
   _____
   _____
   _____
   _____
   _____

2. Describe how you would feel after you did any or all of the preceding activities.

   _____
   _____
   _____
   _____
   _____
   _____
   _____

Exercise VII.B

3. Record *at least* three reasons why you should take care of yourself by engaging in the activities that you identified in item 1.
   A. _____.
   B. _____.
   C. _____.
   D. _____.
   E. _____.

4. Pick a day and time in which you will do at least one of the self-nurturing activities you identified in item 1.

   | Activity | Day | Time |
   | --- | --- | --- |
   |  |  |  |

5. Pick two other days and times to do two other self-nurturing activities that you identified in item 1.

   | Activity | Day | Time |
   | --- | --- | --- |
   |  |  |  |

   | Activity | Day | Time |
   | --- | --- | --- |
   |  |  |  |

6. Describe how you felt after doing the self-nurturing activity.
   _____
   _____.

7. Remind yourself that you needed and deserved time for you. Be good to yourself!

**Therapist's Overview**

# WHAT DRAWER DOES THIS BELONG IN?

## GOALS OF THE EXERCISE

1. Learn the three-drawer approach to prioritizing your responsibilities.
2. Identify which tasks are essential to complete and which can be put off.
3. Decrease feelings of stress that are related to responsibilities as a caregiver.

## ADDITIONAL HOMEWORK THAT MAY BE APPLICABLE TO CAREGIVER BURNOUT

| | | |
|---|---|---|
| • Assertiveness Deficit | It's Okay to Be Assertive | Page 51 |
| • Type-A Stress | Where's My Tension? | Page 263 |
| • Type-A Stress | When I Feel Tension/Stress I Can . . . | Page 266 |

## ADDITIONAL PROBLEMS IN WHICH THIS EXERCISE MAY BE USEFUL

- Adult Children of Alcoholics
- Type-A Stress

## SUGGESTIONS FOR PROCESSING THIS EXERCISE WITH THE CLIENT

Caregivers often add to their own stress level because of having to get things done. However, some of the things they deem as have-tos are really not. The following exercise should be used after you discuss what the three-drawer approach to prioritizing responsibilities involves. The three-drawer approach entails the top drawer for tasks that are essential to daily living, the middle drawer for tasks that can endure a temporary postponement while still avoiding any negative consequences, and the bottom drawer for tasks that can be put off forever.

Exercise VII.C

# WHAT DRAWER DOES THIS BELONG IN?

As a caregiver, you may feel overwhelmed by all of the responsibilities that have been placed on you. It is important and helpful if these responsibilities can be ranked in an order of priority. The three-drawer approach helps you to put each responsibility into its proper drawer. In doing so, you will hopefully feel less overwhelmed.

1. List as many of your daily responsibilities as a caregiver on the following lines.

   _____
   _____
   _____
   _____
   _____

2. For each responsibility, identify the consequence(s) for not completing it on a daily basis.

   | Responsibility | Consequence |
   | --- | --- |
   | _____ | _____ |
   | _____ | _____ |
   | _____ | _____ |
   | _____ | _____ |
   | _____ | _____ |
   | _____ | _____ |
   | _____ | _____ |

3. Write down any responsibility in which there is no consequence.

   _____
   _____
   _____
   _____

Exercise VII.C

4. These responsibilities represent the bottom drawer and do not need to be completed on a daily basis. If you do not get to it, you are still a good and caring person.

5. Write down any responsibility that can be postponed for a few days, or in which the consequence is minimal and is something that you and the person you are taking care of can live with.

_____
_____
_____
_____
_____

6. These responsibilities represent the middle drawer. If you do not get to complete these, you are still a good and caring person.

7. Write down any responsibilities that are absolutely essential that you complete on a daily basis. If these are not completed, the consequence will be life threatening or very severe.

_____
_____
_____
_____
_____

8. These represent the responsibilities that you need to complete every day. To do so, rewrite them in the following blanks, or on another piece of paper and laminate it. Once you complete each responsibility, you can check it off of your list.

| **Responsibility** | **Done** |
|---|---|
| _____ | _____ |
| _____ | _____ |
| _____ | _____ |
| _____ | _____ |
| _____ | _____ |
| _____ | _____ |
| _____ | _____ |
| _____ | _____ |

# Section VIII

# CHEMICAL DEPENDENCE

Therapist's Overview

# I USE BECAUSE . . .

## GOALS OF THE EXERCISE

1. Begin to identify the behavioral, cognitive, and social triggers to one's use.
2. Inform an individual's support network of these triggers to create and allow for greater support.

## ADDITIONAL HOMEWORK THAT MAY BE APPLICABLE TO CHEMICAL DEPENDENCE

- Anger Control Problems   My Safe Place                       Page 33
- Anxiety                  Beating Self-Defeating Beliefs      Page 42
- Caregiver Burnout        Which Drawer Does This Belong In?   Page 74

## ADDITIONAL PROBLEMS IN WHICH THIS EXERCISE MAY BE USEFUL

- Agoraphobia/Panic
- Anger Control Problems
- Anxiety
- Assertiveness Deficit
- Domestic Violence Offenders

## SUGGESTIONS FOR PROCESSING THIS EXERCISE WITH THE CLIENT

For an individual to remain abstinent, he or she must learn to identify the behavioral, cognitive, and social triggers to his/her use. The following exercise will help group members keep track of what these triggers may be. The greater self-awareness an individual develops, the more control and success he/she will have in remaining abstinent. After identifying these triggers, individuals should be encouraged to share what they are with the other group members as well as with any other individual who is a part of that person's support network.

Exercise VIII.A

# I USE BECAUSE...

Remaining abstinent is a tremendous challenge that needs to be met and conquered on a daily basis. To make this task a little easier, it is important to know what situations pose greater risks to you to use. Once you have identified these triggers, you should share them with those who are a part of your support network. Letting them know what makes it tougher for you will help them to help you. Think back about the last three to five times that you used, and answer the following questions.

1. Whom were you with?

2. Where were you?

3. What time of the day was it?

4. Describe the situation. What was going on?

5. How were you feeling before you chose to use?

6. What were you thinking about before you used?

7. What were your thoughts and/or feelings about that person or those people whom you were with?

8. What did the substance do for you?

Exercise VIII.A

9. What were you able to avoid by using (i.e., feelings, hassles, people, situations, responsibilities)?
   _____
   _____

10. What were your thoughts and feelings after you used?
    _____
    _____

11. Based on the preceding information, make a list of the people, places, and things, as well as the feelings you tend to experience, that seem to be triggers for you to use.

| People | Places |
|---|---|
| _____ | _____ |
| _____ | _____ |
| _____ | _____ |
| _____ | _____ |
| _____ | _____ |
| _____ | _____ |
| _____ | _____ |
| _____ | _____ |
| _____ | _____ |

| Things | Feelings |
|---|---|
| _____ | _____ |
| _____ | _____ |
| _____ | _____ |
| _____ | _____ |
| _____ | _____ |
| _____ | _____ |
| _____ | _____ |
| _____ | _____ |

Exercise VIII.A

12. Describe how you feel and what you think about yourself when you are able to abstain from using.

_____
_____
_____
_____
_____

13. Share this exercise with your group and other support people in your life.

Therapist's Overview

# WHAT TO DO INSTEAD OF USING

## GOALS OF THE EXERCISE

1. Identify the people, places, feelings, and things that lead a person to use.
2. Generate a list of alternative activities to engage in when feeling the urge to use.
3. Remain clean and sober.

## ADDITIONAL HOMEWORK THAT MAY BE APPLICABLE TO CHEMICAL DEPENDENCE

| | | |
|---|---|---|
| • Anger Control Problems | My Safe Place | Page 33 |
| • Anxiety | Beating Self-Defeating Beliefs | Page 42 |
| • Bulimia | What Am I Thinking? | Page 62 |
| • Caregiver Burnout | Which Drawer Does This Belong In? | Page 74 |

## ADDITIONAL PROBLEMS IN WHICH THIS EXERCISE MAY BE USEFUL

- Agoraphobia/Panic
- Anger Control Problems
- Anxiety
- Assertiveness Deficit
- Bulimia
- Domestic Violence Offenders

## SUGGESTIONS FOR PROCESSING THIS EXERCISE WITH THE CLIENT

Once the triggers of people, places, feelings, and things have been identified, individuals need to have a list of alternative things to do and think about to prevent relapse. Use the following exercise to have individuals develop that list. Ideally, individuals should complete the "I Use Because . . ." homework exercise prior to completing this assignment.

Exercise VIII.B

# WHAT TO DO INSTEAD OF USING

Once you are aware of the triggers to using, you need to develop a game plan for what to do instead of using. The following exercise will help you to do just that.

1. Refer to your list of people, places, things, and feelings that are triggers to you using.
2. Let's start with your list of people. Next to each person on this list, identify at least one way for you to avoid being alone with him/her.

| People who tend to be triggers to me using | To avoid being around him/her, I will |
|---|---|
| | |
| | |
| | |
| | |
| | |
| | |
| | |

Exercise VIII.B

3. Next to each place listed in the following, identify at least one other place where you can go to spend time and avoid using.

   **Places that I need to avoid so I don't use**

   **A place I can go to feel safe and not use**

   _____     _____
   _____     _____
   _____     _____
   _____     _____
   _____     _____
   _____     _____
   _____     _____

4. Next to each feeling, list one way to experience and deal with that feeling in a positive and healthy way.

   **Feelings that tend to be a trigger to me using**

   **When I feel this way, instead of using I can**

   _____     _____
   _____     _____
   _____     _____
   _____     _____
   _____     _____
   _____     _____
   _____     _____

Exercise VIII.B

5. Things that tend to be triggers to you using refer to anything that does not fall into the three preceding categories (e.g., having an argument with my partner). Next to each "Thing," list one alternative way you plan to prevent yourself from using.

| Things that tend to be triggers to me using | I will prevent myself from using by |
|---|---|
| _____ | _____ |
| _____ | _____ |
| _____ | _____ |
| _____ | _____ |
| _____ | _____ |
| _____ | _____ |
| _____ | _____ |
| _____ | _____ |

6. Each time that you encounter a trigger (person, place, feeling, or thing) and successfully avoid using, acknowledge your strength in doing so. Share this with a support person.

**Therapist's Overview**

# MY ROAD MAP TO RECOVERY

## GOALS OF THE EXERCISE

1. Identify the people and places that will aid an individual in his/her recovery process.
2. Identify the negative and/or distorted thoughts that contribute to relapse, and replace these with alternative, more realistic and self-adaptive thoughts.
4. Identify possible pitfalls to remaining clean and what options and choices a person has to overcome such pitfalls.
5. Remain clean and sober.

## ADDITIONAL HOMEWORK THAT MAY BE APPLICABLE TO CHEMICAL DEPENDENCE

- Anger Control Problems  My Safe Place  Page 33
- Anxiety  Beating Self-Defeating Beliefs  Page 42
- Bulimia  What Am I Thinking?  Page 62
- Caregiver Burnout  Which Drawer Does This Belong In?  Page 74

## ADDITIONAL PROBLEMS IN WHICH THIS EXERCISE MAY BE USEFUL

- Anger Control Problems
- Bulimia
- Child Molester—Adolescent
- Domestic Violence Offenders
- Incest Offenders—Adult

## SUGGESTIONS FOR PROCESSING THIS EXERCISE WITH CLIENT

Often, individuals will have the will but not the way. This exercise is designed to help individuals create their own road map to recovery. Explain to the group that they will be identifying support people in their life, as well as when and how they will contact these individuals. They will also be identifying the cognitive distortions in which they tend to engage and that maintain their addiction. Let them know that the purpose of the assignment is to give them a plan for staying clean.

Exercise VIII.C

# MY ROAD MAP TO RECOVERY

This exercise is set up for you to develop your road map to recovery. Often, it takes more than just will and determination to remain sober. It takes a plan. How am I going to stay sober or clean? Complete the following exercise to figure out what you need.

1. No one can make it in life without the support of others. Accept this fact and think about people who are or who you would like to be part of your support network.
2. Before you contact anyone, make a list of these people and describe at least one reason why he/she would be a positive and supportive person for you.

| Person | Reason he/she would be a positive and supportive person |
|---|---|
| _____ | _____ |
| _____ | _____ |
| _____ | _____ |
| _____ | _____ |
| _____ | _____ |
| _____ | _____ |
| _____ | _____ |
| _____ | _____ |

3. Review the preceding list. Cross off any person's name with which you feel uncomfortable, and add any others that you think of and feel confident that he/she would be a positive and supportive person. Contact each of these people and explain to them that you are looking for people who can support you on your road to recovery and abstinence. If they agree that you can count on them, write their name in the following list. Record their phone number so that you have a way to get in touch with them when you need to.

Exercise VIII.C

| Person | Phone number |
|---|---|
| _____ | _____ |
| _____ | _____ |
| _____ | _____ |
| _____ | _____ |
| _____ | _____ |
| _____ | _____ |
| _____ | _____ |
| _____ | _____ |
| _____ | _____ |

4. You may want to rewrite these names and phone numbers on something that you can carry with you at all times.

5. Identify times when you think you will need to contact someone from your support network based on certain feelings and/or emotions.

   I should contact someone from my support network whenever I am feeling _____
   _____
   _____
   _____.

6. It is important to recognize the role that our thoughts play in helping us to stay clean and sober or that contribute to our relapse. Think about the times you have used in the past. Try to identify some of the thoughts that would go through your mind and that would decrease your strength and ability to stay abstinent (e.g., "I've been doing so well I deserve to have one drink; besides, one drink won't matter," or "I am so stressed out nothing else has ever worked. One drink (one hit) is all I need and then I can go back to not using at all," or "I just don't care anymore, what's the use?"). Record what has gone through your mind in the past. After each thought, write a thought that would counter or challenge the negative thought (e.g., "One drink is all it takes for me to go right back to the way it was. I like being in control of my life and if I drink even one I will lose my control, my life, and the people who matter to me," or "I am really feeling stressed out and I need some relief. I need to call a support person or my sponsor, someone who can understand or who will listen," or "I will care about myself. I know that bad times are a part of life. But I also know that there is always a tomorrow and that bad times don't last forever").

Exercise VIII.C

Negative thought: _____

Counterthought: _____

Negative thought: _____

Counterthought: _____

Negative thought: _____

Counterthought: _____

Negative thought: _____

Counterthought: _____

Negative thought: _____

Counterthought: _____

Negative thought: _____

Counterthought: _____

Negative thought: _____

Counterthought: _____

Negative thought: _____

Counterthought: _____

Exercise VIII.C

7. Our behavior plays a major role in our road to recovery, just like our thoughts. It is important to identify what we can do to stay clean or sober. Make a list of at least 15 positive activities in which you can engage, on a regular basis, to help you avoid using.

   A. _____
   B. _____
   C. _____
   D. _____
   E. _____
   F. _____
   G. _____
   H. _____
   I. _____
   J. _____
   K. _____
   L. _____
   M. _____
   N. _____
   O. _____
   P. _____
   Q. _____
   R. _____
   S. _____
   T. _____

8. Review this list with your support network.

9. One other important aspect to staying on the road to recovery is knowing why you should stay clean and sober. Identify at least 10 reasons why you should remain clean and sober.

   A. _____
   B. _____
   C. _____
   D. _____
   E. _____
   F. _____

Exercise VIII.C

G. _____
H. _____
I. _____
J. _____
K. _____
L. _____

10. Review this entire assignment with your group and/or people in your support network.

## Section IX

# CHILD SEXUAL MOLESTATION

Therapist's Overview

# THIS IS WHAT HAPPENED

## GOALS OF THE EXERCISE

1. Recognize the need to be honest in order for treatment to be effective and useful.
2. Identify what happened that led up to you committing the offense.
3. Begin to take responsibility for one's sexually inappropriate behavior.
4. Begin to identify possible triggers to offending.

## ADDITIONAL HOMEWORK THAT MAY BE APPLICABLE TO SEXUAL OFFENDING

- Anger Control Problems — Anger Log — Page 24
- Anxiety — Beating Self-Defeating Beliefs — Page 42
- Chemical Dependence — What to Do Instead of Using — Page 82

## ADDITIONAL PROBLEMS IN WHICH THIS EXERCISE MAY BE USEFUL

- Anger Control Problems
- Domestic Violence Offenders

## SUGGESTIONS FOR PROCESSING THIS EXERCISE WITH THE CLIENT

This exercise is designed to help individuals begin to take responsibility for their behavior. Use this exercise at the beginning of treatment to identify the events that may have led up to and contributed to offending.

Exercise IX.A

# THIS IS WHAT HAPPENED

You will be able to use this exercise to describe what was going on before you offended. Be as honest as you can. The sooner you can describe what you did, the sooner you will be able to take full responsibility for your behavior and move on with your life.

1. Whom did you offend?

2. How old was he/she?

3. How old were you when you offended him/her?

4. Where did you offend him/her?

5. Describe the room or area in as much detail as you can (e.g., Were there any windows? How many? What color were the walls? What furniture was in the room?).

6. What made you choose that place?

7. Who else was with you or nearby?

8. How did you know your victim?

9. What did you say to your victim to get him/her to go along with you?

Exercise IX.A

10. Describe your mood before you offended.
   _____

11. Identify any stressors (e.g., work, school, home, family) that you were experiencing before you offended.
   _____
   _____
   _____
   _____

12. When did you first start thinking about offending this person?
   _____

13. What thoughts did you have just before you offended?
   _____
   _____
   _____
   _____

14. How did you feel after you offended?
   _____
   _____

**Therapist's Overview**

# THIS IS WHAT I DID

## GOALS OF THE EXERCISE

1. Recognize the need to be honest in order for treatment to be effective and useful.
2. Identify what happened when you were offending.
3. Identify the thoughts and feelings that you were experiencing.
4. Begin to take responsibility for your sexually inappropriate behavior.
5. Begin to identify possible triggers to offending.

## ADDITIONAL HOMEWORK THAT MAY BE APPLICABLE TO SEXUAL OFFENDING

| | | |
|---|---|---|
| • Anger Control Problems | Anger Log | Page 24 |
| • Anxiety | Beating Self-Defeating Beliefs | Page 42 |
| • Chemical Dependence | What to Do Instead of Using | Page 82 |

## ADDITIONAL PROBLEMS IN WHICH THIS EXERCISE MAY BE USEFUL

- Anger Control Problems
- Domestic Violence Offenders
- Incest Offenders—Adult

## SUGGESTIONS FOR PROCESSING THIS EXERCISE WITH THE CLIENT

This exercise focuses on individuals being able to describe what actually happened when he/she offended. It can be used throughout the process of treatment, because as treatment progresses, clients will often become more honest and open up more. Encourage each person to be as honest as he/she can.

Exercise IX.B

# THIS IS WHAT I DID

The following exercise is for you to describe in detail what you did. In describing this, you will be able to get a sense of what you were thinking about and feeling before, during, and after you offended.

1. What time of day was it when you offended (or when you usually abused your victim)?

2. What did you say to _____ (write in your victim's name) to get him/her to go along with you?

3. Before you approached _____ (write in your victim's name), what were you saying to yourself that justified what you were planning to do?

4. Describe the type of mood or feelings that you were experiencing before you offended.

5. What did you do or say to engage _____ (write in your victim's name) in the sexually inappropriate (abusive) behavior?

6. What did _____ (write in your victim's name) say or do?

7. How do you think _____ (write in your victim's name) was feeling at this point?

Exercise IX.B

8. What do you think _____ (write in your victim's name) was thinking?
   _____
   _____

9. Imagine that you are watching a movie in slow motion. Picture offending _____ (victim's name).

   How did you touch _____ (victim's name)? _____
   _____
   _____

   How did you have _____ (victim's name) touch you? _____
   _____
   _____

   What was _____ (victim's name) reaction? _____
   _____
   _____

   What were you thinking about when you were touching_____
   (victim's name) or being touched by _____ (victim's name)? _____
   _____
   _____

   How did you feel when you were doing this?
   _____
   _____

   How did you restrain _____ (victim's name)? If not physically, how did you verbally intimidate him/her?
   _____
   _____

   How did you stop? How did _____ (victim's name) know you were done? What did you say or do?
   _____
   _____

   How did _____ (victim's name) feel at this point?
   _____
   _____

**Exercise IX.B**

What do you think _____ (victim's name) was thinking about?
_____
_____

What were you thinking about when you stopped?
_____
_____

How did you feel about yourself after you stopped abusing _____ (victim's name)?
_____

How did you feel about _____ (victim's name) after you stopped?
_____
_____

How did you get _____ (victim's name) to not say anything about what you did?
_____
_____

**Therapist's Overview**

# I'M CHANGING THE WAY I THINK

## GOALS OF THE EXERCISE

1. Identify sexual fantasies that are inappropriate.
2. Recognize the thinking errors that you use to justify inappropriate sexual fantasies and behaviors.
3. Develop reality-based thoughts that facilitate a healthy frame of mind and that can encourage positive and appropriate behavior.
4. Begin to take responsibility for one's sexually inappropriate behavior.
5. Begin to identify possible triggers to offending.

## ADDITIONAL HOMEWORK THAT MAY BE APPLICABLE TO SEXUAL OFFENDING

- Anger Control Problems      Anger Log                         Page 24
- Anxiety                     Beating Self-Defeating Beliefs    Page 42
- Chemical Dependence         What to Do Instead of Using       Page 82

## ADDITIONAL PROBLEMS IN WHICH THIS EXERCISE MAY BE USEFUL

- Anger Control Problems
- Domestic Violence Offenders
- Incest Offenders—Adult

## SUGGESTIONS FOR PROCESSING THIS EXERCISE WITH THE CLIENT

An individual who commits a sexual offense, whether he/she is an adolescent or adult, needs to identify the thinking errors that allow and justify the cycle of offending to continue. In this exercise, individuals will be asked to keep a journal of daily thoughts and behaviors. They will evaluate their daily life for thinking errors and possible triggers to offending. They will also develop alternative thoughts and activities to create a positive cycle of behavior versus an offending cycle. Before assigning this homework, be sure to review the various types of thinking errors in which a person can engage to justify sexual offending.

Exercise IX.C

# I'M CHANGING THE WAY I THINK

This exercise is to aid you in evaluating your daily life for possible thinking errors and other triggers that may lead you to reoffend. You will need to work on this every day, and it will take you about 15 to 20 minutes each time. Being able to genuinely complete this exercise will demonstrate your willingness to take responsibility for your actions and desire to change.

Date: _____

1. Describe your day. Be sure to include any feelings of stress or negative feelings and/or thoughts about yourself.

   _____
   _____
   _____
   _____
   _____
   _____
   _____
   _____

2. Describe any sexual thoughts that you had today. Include the age of the person about whom you were thinking, what he/she looked like, what he/she was doing, and what you were doing. Describe how you felt and how you thought he/she would have felt.

   _____
   _____
   _____
   _____
   _____
   _____
   _____
   _____

Exercise IX.C

3. Identify the thinking errors you engaged in (e.g., "It was just a fantasy, I didn't really do anything, no one got hurt," or "She really liked me staring at her").

   _____
   _____
   _____
   _____
   _____
   _____
   _____
   _____

4. For each thinking error, write an alternative thought that is more reality-based and positive (e.g., "The more I think this way, the more likely it is that I will behave this way. I don't want to do that," or "I am a good person and I don't need to act this way to feel good or strong").

   _____
   _____
   _____
   _____
   _____
   _____
   _____
   _____

Therapist's Overview

# STOP! REWIND! AND START AGAIN

## GOALS OF THE EXERCISE

1. Identify thinking errors or inappropriate sexual thoughts and/or fantasies.
2. Practice thought-stopping techniques to reduce and possibly eliminate the thinking errors or inappropriate sexual thoughts and/or fantasies.
3. Develop reality-based thoughts that facilitate a healthy frame of mind and that can encourage positive and appropriate behavior.
4. Begin to take responsibility for one's sexually inappropriate thoughts and behavior.

## ADDITIONAL HOMEWORK THAT MAY BE APPLICABLE TO SEXUAL OFFENDING

- Anger Control Problems — Anger Log — Page 24
- Anxiety — Beating Self-Defeating Beliefs — Page 42
- Chemical Dependence — What to Do Instead of Using — Page 82

## ADDITIONAL PROBLEMS IN WHICH THIS EXERCISE MAY BE USEFUL

- Anger Control Problems
- Chemical Dependence
- Incest Offenders—Adult

## SUGGESTIONS FOR PROCESSING THIS EXERCISE WITH THE CLIENT

Thinking errors contribute greatly to offending behavior. Therefore, individuals need to learn ways to redirect or replace such thoughts. Explain that reducing and redirecting such thoughts are only part of recovery, but they're a big part.

Exercise IX.D

# STOP! REWIND! AND START AGAIN

It is difficult to stop thinking a certain way, especially if you have done so for a long time. However, in most situations, the way we think strongly influences the way we act and feel about things. You probably know that your thoughts played a significant role in your offending behavior. Therefore, it is important to recognize when your thoughts are sexually inappropriate or negative. Once you recognize such thoughts, you then need to find ways to redirect or replace them. This exercise will help you to learn ways to redirect and replace sexually inappropriate thoughts and thinking errors.

1. To recognize when you are engaging in sexually inappropriate or negative thinking, you need to become aware of when you typically do this. There are many ways to figure this out. One way is to track your thoughts on a regular basis. For example, every hour of the day, take a minute to write down whatever you are thinking about. If this is not realistic to do, then perhaps you can write down your thoughts before you go to school or work in the morning, at lunchtime, and after dinner. Buy a journal or a notebook to keep track of these thoughts.

2. You may already know that when you see someone who fits a certain profile you become sexually interested in him/her. This could be a trigger to inappropriate thoughts. Try to think of any other situations or triggers that would lead to inappropriate sexual thoughts.

    Triggers or situations that tend to cause me to start thinking inappropriate thoughts:

    _____
    _____
    _____
    _____
    _____
    _____
    _____

3. Once you have a handle on when and what situations or triggers lead you into having inappropriate sexual thoughts, you can then begin to plan for ways to redirect or replace such thinking.

Exercise IX.D

4. Every person is different and what works for one person may not work for you. It is important to figure out what strategies do work the most.

5. Here are several ways for you to redirect or replace unwanted thoughts.
   - Shout "STOP" in your head or aloud.
   - Keep a rubber band on your wrist and snap it every time you have an unwanted thought.
   - Visualize a stop sign.
   - If a stop sign is not enough, picture getting caught, or going to jail, or something similar.
   - Make a list of the reasons why you should not have such thoughts, and review this list daily or as frequently as you need.
   - Carry a picture of yourself in jail or in a juvenile detention center.
   - Carry a copy of the news clipping describing what you did as a reminder of how it felt when you got caught.
   - Write about how it felt to get caught and for everyone to know what you did. Keep this with you or review it frequently.
   - Imagine how someone you respect and admire would feel about you if he/she knew what you were thinking.
   - Because you are smart and know yourself better than anyone else, you may know of other strategies that would also work to redirect or replace your inappropriate thoughts. Use the following lines to describe what else you could do.

   _____
   _____
   _____
   _____
   _____
   _____
   _____
   _____

6. Practice the strategies just described and rate the effectiveness of each. On the following lines, list the top four or five strategies that have worked the best for you.
   A. _____
   B. _____
   C. _____
   D. _____
   E. _____
   F. Once you have practiced these strategies, you will no longer need to STOP! REWIND! AND START AGAIN—they will become automatic.

**Section X**

# CHRONIC PAIN

Therapist's Overview

# AAH! RELIEF, WRITTEN AND DIRECTED BY _____
(WRITE IN YOUR NAME)

## GOALS OF THE EXERCISE

1. Practice visual imagery techniques and progressive muscle relaxation techniques to reduce pain.
2. Develop some control over chronic pain and ways to experience relief.

## ADDITIONAL HOMEWORK THAT MAY BE APPLICABLE TO CHRONIC PAIN

- Depression        Taking Charge of Your Thoughts        Page 126
- HIV/AIDS          Why Me?                               Page 161

## ADDITIONAL PROBLEMS IN WHICH THIS EXERCISE MAY BE USEFUL

- Anxiety
- Depression
- HIV/AIDS
- Incest Survivors—Adult
- Rape Survivors

## SUGGESTIONS FOR PROCESSING THIS EXERCISE WITH THE CLIENT

This exercise is designed to help individuals to learn and practice progressive muscle relaxation and visual imagery techniques as a way to reduce their chronic pain. Individuals should practice both the progressive muscle relaxation and visualization in a session before doing so at home. For the visualization, have individuals describe what their pain looks like (e.g., "My back is one big knot," or "My head feels like it is caught in a vice grip"). Once they have identified what the pain looks like, have them describe the pain being released (e.g., "The knot slowly unties itself," or "The vice grip loosens and falls away").

Exercise X.A

# AAH! RELIEF, WRITTEN AND DIRECTED BY _____
(WRITE IN YOUR NAME)

Dealing with chronic pain can be agonizing. Think of what it would be like without the pain. Think of what it would be like if you could control and determine when and to what degree you have pain. Overcoming the pain takes a lot of determination. Something that is as powerful as the pain and that is available to each of us is our mind. Using our minds to visualize peace in our lives and to control our bodily reactions can have great success in overcoming pain. This is more easily said than done, however. Making this more realistic requires a positive attitude and practice. In the end, you will begin to be able to take control over the pain (instead of vice versa) and to find some relief. On a daily basis, or as often as needed, complete the following:

1. Imagine yourself as the director of a movie. You get to decide what happens and when. The movie that you have just been hired to direct is based on your pain. Picture your pain on the movie screen. Imagine it being outside of your body and up on the screen. Try to describe what it looks like (e.g., "My back is caught in a vice grip").

   _____
   _____

2. Begin to practice deep abdominal breathing and proceed to progressive muscle relaxation.

3. While doing the deep breathing and muscle relaxation, picture as vividly as possible your pain going away (e.g., the vice grip loosening and falling away). You are the director of the movie, describe what you want to see happen.

4. Imagine yourself as feeling and growing healthy and strong. Describe what you would be doing.

   _____
   _____

Exercise X.A

5. How does the movie end?
   _____
   _____
   _____

6. Share this with the others in your group.

Therapist's Overview

# I CAN GET THROUGH THIS

## GOALS OF THE EXERCISE

1. Identify negative thoughts regarding the pain.
2. Practice thought stopping techniques and cognitive restructuring.
3. Develop a list of alternative coping thoughts/statements.

## ADDITIONAL HOMEWORK THAT MAY BE APPLICABLE TO CHRONIC PAIN

- Depression         Taking Charge of Your Thoughts         Page 126
- HIV/AIDS           Why Me?                                 Page 161

## ADDITIONAL PROBLEMS IN WHICH THIS EXERCISE MAY BE USEFUL

- Agoraphobia/Panic
- Anxiety
- Depression

## SUGGESTIONS FOR PROCESSING THIS EXERCISE WITH THE CLIENT

Individuals experiencing chronic pain need to redirect and replace the negative thoughts in which they engage when experiencing pain. These thoughts can increase the physical, as well as the emotional, pain (e.g., anxiety, hopelessness) that they experience. It is important for these individuals to learn skills that attack such negative thinking styles.

**Exercise X.B**

# I CAN GET THROUGH THIS

Most people who experience pain wish that it would go away, as I am sure you have probably done. With chronic pain, people sometimes begin to believe "This will never get better." This can progress to thoughts such as "Life sucks" or "Life is not worth living." We could perhaps add pages to this list. The point, however, is that such thoughts can actually add more pain to what you are already feeling. More pain is not something you need, right? Therefore, it is important to identify the types of thoughts you have when you are feeling the pain. Now you might say, "I have pain all the time." That's true, but sometimes the pain is more manageable. Typically, when the pain is unmanageable, people's thoughts tend to be more negative. The following exercise is designed to help you to identify when your thoughts are negative and counterproductive to your being able to manage the pain.

1. Make a list of the negative thoughts in which you tend to engage. You may need to keep track of this for a week to get a better idea of what those negative thoughts are.

   When the pain is unmanageable, the negative thoughts in which I tend to engage include:

   _____
   _____
   _____
   _____
   _____
   _____
   _____
   _____
   _____
   _____
   _____
   _____
   _____

Exercise X.B

2. Now make a list of positive and/or alternative thoughts you could say to yourself that would be more hopeful (e.g., "I can cope with this, I've gotten through it before").

___

3. Whenever you are engaging in negative thoughts, learn to stop yourself and replace them with the statements you have listed in item 2.
4. Some ways for you to stop and redirect yourself from the negative thoughts include:
    - Shout "STOP" in your head or aloud.
    - Keep a rubber band on your wrist and snap it every time you have an unwanted thought.
    - Visualize a stop sign.
5. You can, and should, add to the list of ways to stop and redirect negative thoughts.
6. Read the positive thoughts you listed in item 2 frequently throughout every day.

# Section XI

# CODEPENDENCE

Therapist's Overview

# I'M NOT IN KANSAS ANYMORE

## GOALS OF THE EXERCISE

1. Identify times and situations in which individuals feel like they are losing themselves.
2. Begin to describe, understand, and establish personal boundaries.
3. Practice setting limits and boundaries.

## ADDITIONAL HOMEWORK THAT MAY BE APPLICABLE TO CODEPENDENCE

- Adult Children of Alcoholics — What's My Role? — Page 3
- Adult Children of Alcoholics — What Can I Control? What Do I Need? — Page 6
- Assertiveness Deficit — It's Okay to Be Assertive — Page 51
- Caregiver Burnout — This Is for Me and That's Okay — Page 71

## ADDITIONAL PROBLEMS IN WHICH THIS EXERCISE MAY BE USEFUL

- Adult Children of Alcoholics
- Assertiveness Deficit

## SUGGESTIONS FOR PROCESSING THIS EXERCISE WITH THE CLIENT

By definition, individuals who are codependent have great difficulty with boundaries. Often, these individuals will describe a sense of losing oneself because they do not create and maintain personal boundaries. The purpose of the following exercise is to help individuals who are characteristically codependent to learn the benefits of developing and establishing boundaries.

Exercise XI.A

# I'M NOT IN KANSAS ANYMORE

Have you ever experienced the sense that you are not sure when you stop and someone or something else begins? When we lose sight of our personal boundaries, or if we have not defined and established personal boundaries, we often feel like we've lost ourselves. Who am I? What do I like to do? When can I do something for me and just me, without having to worry about, or feel like I have to control, someone or some situation? To maintain a sense of self, it is essential that each of us develops and puts into practice personal boundaries. The purpose of the following exercise is to help you to identify, describe, and understand, as well as put into place, your personal boundaries.

1. Think of several situations in which you've felt like you've lost your sense of self. One example is this. "When my husband comes home and asks me 50 questions about my day and I am not in the mood to talk, I start to shut down. I then begin to feel overwhelmed because I can't get him to stop, and I can't speak to tell him to slow down or to stop. That's when I just feel like I lose myself and begin to function on autopilot. I am really not even there." Another example is this. "Every time we go out, I agree to do what you want because I usually like what you like. But once, it would be nice if I could say what I want to do without feeling guilty or having to also do what you want to do." Describe at least three situations in which you have felt like you've lost your sense of self.

   _____
   _____
   _____
   _____
   _____
   _____
   _____

2. It is important to recognize common situations in which you feel like you've lost that sense of "me"ness. Over the next week, keep a journal of times when you experience this feeling and describe what happened.

   Sunday: _____
   _____
   _____

Exercise XI.A

Monday: _____
_____
_____

Tuesday: _____
_____
_____

Wednesday: _____
_____
_____

Thursday: _____
_____
_____

Friday: _____
_____
_____

Saturday: _____
_____
_____

3. For each situation in which you felt that sense of losing yourself, describe what you could have done or would like to have done differently. An example: "When I was talking over the phone with my daughter, she started to complain about her life but would not listen to any of my suggestions. I started to feel overwhelmed and so wrapped up in her life and in fixing her problems that I started to lose myself. The next time that this happens I could say, 'I'm sorry, honey, someone is ringing in on the other line, I'll have to call you back later.' " This will help preserve *you* and give you a break from feeling sucked in or overwhelmed.

_____
_____
_____
_____
_____
_____
_____
_____

4. Review your answers in item 3 several times a day. This will keep them fresh in your mind and help you to put them into practice.

Therapist's Overview

# I FEEL . . .

## GOALS OF THE EXERCISE

1. Begin to verbalize feelings using "I" statements.
2. Increase assertiveness skills and maintain boundaries.
3. Practice setting limits and boundaries, and be aware of the feelings that one experiences when boundaries are kept.

## ADDITIONAL HOMEWORK THAT MAY BE APPLICABLE TO CODEPENDENCE

- Adult Children of Alcoholics     What's My Role?                               Page 3
- Adult Children of Alcoholics     What Can I Control? What Do I Need?           Page 6
- Assertiveness Deficit            It's Okay to Be Assertive                     Page 51
- Caregiver Burnout                This Is for Me and That's Okay                Page 71

## ADDITIONAL PROBLEMS IN WHICH THIS EXERCISE MAY BE USEFUL

- Adult Children of Alcoholics
- Anger Control Problems
- Assertiveness Deficit
- Domestic Violence Offenders

## SUGGESTIONS FOR PROCESSING THIS EXERCISE WITH THE CLIENT

This exercise is similar to the "I'm Not in Kansas Anymore" assignment. Individuals will learn to identify specific boundaries and limits that they need to establish on a regular basis. In addition, individuals will learn to practice using "I" statements, which will help to reinforce the sense of self, being important and present.

Exercise XI.B

# I FEEL . . .

Most of us do not say how we feel when we should and to whom we should say it. This exercise will help you change that. It involves several steps. Take each step one at a time.

**Step 1.** For the next three days, check in with yourself regarding how you are feeling. Every hour or two jot down whatever feeling you are experiencing. It would be best if you used a small notebook. The following list of feeling words will help.

| | | | | | |
|---|---|---|---|---|---|
| Mad | Irritable | Annoyed | On edge | Stressed | Crabby |
| Enraged | Frustrated | Pissed (off) | Furious | Afraid | Worried |
| Nervous | Concerned | Uncertain | Distrustful | Scared | Confused |
| Shocked | Uneasy | Frazzled | Tense | Cautious | Doubtful |
| Sad | Lonely | Alone | Unloved | Unhappy | Blue<br>Depressed |
| Rejected | Blah | Moody | Upset | Hopeless | Overwhelmed |
| Ashamed | Guilty | Embarrassed | Vulnerable | Stupid<br>Inadequate | Hurt<br>Disappointed |
| Disapproved | Jealous | Glad | Joyous | Energetic<br>Happy<br>Enthusiastic | Hopeful |
| Relieved | Cheerful | Excited | Loved<br>Wanted | Cared for | Peaceful |
| Proud | Secure<br>Confident | Safe | Grounded | Accepted | Pleased |

Here is an example of how you could track your feelings.

Date/day: _____ Time: _____ Feeling: _____

Date/day: _____ Time: _____ Feeling: _____

Date/day: _____ Time: _____ Feeling: _____

Date/day: _____ Time: _____ Feeling: _____

**Exercise XI.B**

**Step 2.** Over the next two days, tell someone how you are feeling at least four different times. Be clear and specific. For example, "I felt uncomfortable and taken advantage of when you invited people over without talking to me about it first." Try to pick different people each time.

**Step 3.** While you are expressing how you feel, think about how things might be if you did not say how you were feeling. Would you have been feeling overwhelmed or frustrated? In stating how you feel, are you describing or putting in place any boundaries? If you are developing new boundaries, describe them. For example, "Since I told my _____ that I feel awkward and uncomfortable about him/her just inviting people over without first talking with me, I have started to establish a boundary regarding my home and who comes in and when."

_____
_____
_____
_____
_____
_____

Now that you have had some practice in using "I" statements to describe how you are feeling, make it a habit.

**Step 4.** Each day, use an "I" statement to describe how you are feeling at least two different times a day. Record if you are establishing any new boundaries, as well as if you are reinforcing any other ones. You should also add a note to yourself regarding how you are feeling about yourself in being able to speak up for yourself and express your feelings.

# Section XII

# DEPRESSION

Therapist's Overview

# WHAT DO OTHERS VALUE ABOUT ME?*

## GOALS OF THE EXERCISE

1. Develop a sense of value.
2. Develop a stronger sense of self-worth.

## ADDITIONAL HOMEWORK THAT MAY BE APPLICABLE TO DEPRESSION

- Adult Children of Alcoholics     What's My Role?     Page 3
- Anger Control Problems     My Safe Place     Page 33
- Anxiety     Beating Self-Defeating Beliefs     Page 42

## ADDITIONAL PROBLEMS IN WHICH THIS EXERCISE MAY BE USEFUL

- Anxiety
- Anger
- Assertiveness Deficit

## SUGGESTIONS FOR PROCESSING THIS EXERCISE WITH THE CLIENT

Many individuals suffering with depression find little value in themselves. They tend to have low self-esteem or low self-worth. This exercise provides them an opportunity to challenge that view and belief. They will need to ask other individuals, whom they feel close to or care about, to describe some characteristics and qualities that they value about him/her. Let them know that this might feel a little awkward, but to do it anyway. Assure them that they can.

---

*This exercise was first described by Bevilacqua, L., & Dattilio, F. (2001) *Brief Family Therapy Homework Planner.* New York: John Wiley & Sons.

Exercise XII.A

# WHAT DO OTHERS VALUE ABOUT ME?

Many individuals who suffer with depression report feeling a lack of value. One of the ways for you to generate more positive feelings and thoughts about yourself, which will promote positive self-esteem and self-worth, is to gather support regarding what a good person you really are. To do this, you will need to ask a few people you feel close to and feel comfortable with, to describe what they value about you. Although you may feel a little awkward in asking, ask anyway. Record their feedback.

1. _____ said that he/she values me because _____
   _____.

2. _____ said that he/she values me because _____
   _____.

3. _____ said that he/she values me because _____
   _____.

4. _____ said that he/she values me because _____
   _____.

Therapist's Overview

# MY FEELINGS JOURNAL

## GOALS OF THE EXERCISE

1. Identify times and situations that you tend to feel depressed.
2. Increase skills of self-monitoring.
3. Identify thoughts and behaviors as they relate to your feelings.

## ADDITIONAL HOMEWORK THAT MAY BE APPLICABLE TO DEPRESSION

- Adult Children of Alcoholics — What's My Role? — Page 3
- Anger Control Problems — My Safe Place — Page 33
- Anxiety — Beating Self-Defeating Beliefs — Page 42

## ADDITIONAL PROBLEMS IN WHICH THIS EXERCISE MAY BE USEFUL

- Anger Control Problems
- Anxiety
- Incest Survivors—Adult
- Toxic Parent Survivors

## SUGGESTIONS FOR PROCESSING THIS EXERCISE WITH THE CLIENT

Many people have difficulty identifying and expressing their feelings. Individuals who are depressed will often withhold their feelings. It is important for all of us to be able to express what we are feeling. The purpose of this exercise is to help individuals identify and describe their feelings, especially when they are feeling depressed. In addition, individuals will learn to identify their thoughts and behaviors. In doing so, you will be able to identify patterns as well as understand how feelings, thoughts, and behaviors influence each other. The more an individual is aware of his/her thoughts and behaviors regarding his/her feelings, the more empowered he/she can be to make changes.

Exercise XII.B

# MY FEELINGS JOURNAL

This exercise will help you to identify and describe how you feel throughout the day. You will also learn to be more aware of your thoughts and behaviors and how they influence and affect your feelings. The more you are aware of your thoughts and behaviors regarding your feelings, the more equipped you can be to make changes.

1. Throughout the day, perhaps at breakfast, lunch, and dinner, practice asking yourself how you feel. Write that feeling down and then record whatever is going through your mind and what you are doing. Don't try to interpret anything, just get in touch with your feelings and take notice to your thoughts and behaviors. Use the following list of feeling words to help you identify your feelings.

| Mad | Irritable | Annoyed | On edge | Stressed | Crabby |
|---|---|---|---|---|---|
| Enraged | Frustrated | Pissed (off) | Furious | Afraid | Worried |
| Nervous | Concerned | Uncertain | Distrustful | Scared | Confused |
| Shocked | Uneasy | Frazzled | Tense | Cautious | Doubtful |
| Sad | Lonely | Alone | Unloved | Unhappy | Blue Depressed |
| Rejected | Blah | Moody | Upset | Hopeless | Overwhelmed |
| Ashamed | Guilty Embarrassed | Vulnerable | Stupid Inadequate | Hurt | Disappointed |
| Disapproved | Jealous | Glad Joyous | Happy | Enthusiastic | Energetic |
| Hopeful | Relieved | Cheerful | Excited | Loved Wanted | Cared for |
| Peaceful | Proud Secure Confident | Safe | Grounded | Accepted | Pleased |

You can use the following format to track your feelings, thoughts and behaviors. Do this three times each day.

Date and time: _____

I am feeling _____.

I am thinking _____

_____.

Exercise XII.B

I am doing _____
_____.

2. Keep this journal for at least one week.
3. After you have recorded in your journal for at least one week, reread it and look for themes or patterns. Try to fill in the following sentence stems.

When I felt depressed (down, blue, upset, sad, etc.) my thoughts tended to be (e.g., negative, such as, "I can't . . .," or "Nothing ever goes right for me") _____
_____
_____.

When I felt _____ and had such thoughts, I tended to (describe typical behavior)
_____
_____.

When I felt happy (cheerful, good, excited, etc.) my thoughts tended to be _____
_____
_____.

When I felt _____ and had such thoughts, I tended to (describe typical behavior)
_____
_____.

When I felt mad (angry, resentful, frustrated, etc.) my thoughts tended to be _____
_____
_____.

When I felt _____ and had such thoughts, I tended to (describe typical behavior)
_____
_____.

When I felt scared (worried, nervous, etc.) my thoughts tended to be _____
_____
_____.

When I felt _____ and had such thoughts, I tended to (describe typical behavior)
_____
_____.

When I felt _____ my thoughts tended to be _____
_____
_____.

When I felt _____ and had such thoughts, I tended to (describe typical behavior)
_____
_____.

Therapist's Overview

# TAKING CHARGE OF YOUR THOUGHTS

## GOALS OF THE EXERCISE

1. Identify times and situations that you tend to feel depressed.
2. Identify the thinking errors that tend to create and maintain feeling depressed.
3. Identify alternative and more positive, reality-based thoughts.
4. Increase skills of self-monitoring.

## ADDITIONAL HOMEWORK THAT MAY BE APPLICABLE TO DEPRESSION

- Adult Children of Alcoholics    What's My Role?    Page 3
- Anger Control Problems    My Safe Place    Page 33
- Anxiety    Beating Self-Defeating Beliefs    Page 42

## ADDITIONAL PROBLEMS IN WHICH THIS EXERCISE MAY BE USEFUL

- Anxiety
- Anger
- Bulimia and other types of eating disorders

## SUGGESTIONS FOR PROCESSING THIS EXERCISE WITH THE CLIENT

Once individuals recognize that they are suffering from depression, they need to learn not only what creates and maintains it but what to do about it. The following exercise will help individuals identify the various types of cognitive distortions or thinking errors they engage in. Because the way we think can greatly influence a person's level of depression, it is important for people to identify what they tend to say to themselves when they are feeling down or depressed. Once they take the first step of identifying these distortions or thinking errors, they can then learn a variety of strategies to effectively overcome feeling down or depressed.

Exercise XII.C

# TAKING CHARGE OF YOUR THOUGHTS

The following exercise is designed to help you recognize how your thoughts sometimes create and maintain your feelings of depression. You will also have a chance to try various strategies for overcoming your feelings of depression.

1. Review the definition and example for each of the following thinking errors (that many people make) and see which ones you tend to engage in.

    **Catastrophizing.**  This is when you think about consequences and you blow them out of proportion in a negative way. For example, while baking you leave the cookies in the oven a minute longer than planned. You react by saying, "I might as well throw this whole batch out and just buy a box already made. I am such a lousy baker."

    **Overgeneralization.**  This is when you think of one example to make conclusions about a number of other things, or all similar circumstances. In the example of baking cookies, an overgeneralization would be, "I should just stay out of the kitchen because I can never cook anything well."

    **Fortune-telling.**  This is when you predict that negative things will happen to you in the future with little or no evidence to support your prediction. For example, you get angry with your spouse and think to yourself, "Why bother telling him, he won't listen anyway."

    **Black-and-white thinking.**  This is when you look at situations, others, or even yourself as totally bad or totally good—without thinking about the in between, or, gray area. For example, "If you don't like me, you must hate me."

    **Dark glasses or mental filtering.**  This is when you block out the positives and just focus on the negatives. For example, Mike met with his boss for his annual job review. His boss pointed out many positive aspects of Mike's work but suggested he try to improve on one area. In reflecting back on the meeting, Mike could only think about the aspect he needed to improve on and felt like he was doing a poor job.

    **Personalizing.**  This is when you take on the responsibility for something that is not your job. For example, Sondra arranged to have pizza delivered to her house for a party she was having. The delivery person got lost and never arrived with the pizza. She thought to herself, "I should have never called that place, why couldn't I have called the other pizza store? Can't I do anything right?"

**Discounting.** This is when you reject the positive things that happen to you. For example, Michelle's girlfriend told Michelle that her outfit looks great, but Michelle thought to herself, "This outfit looks terrible on me, she is just trying to say something nice, but doesn't really mean it."

**Judging.** This is when you are critical of yourself or others and make statements such as, "I should be more relaxed," I ought to know by now," "I have to get this right."

**Mind-reading.** This is when you make a negative assumption regarding other people's thoughts and behaviors. For example, Bryan passed a girl in the hall and when she did not say hello to him he thought, "She hates me, I don't stand a chance with her."

*Before you proceed, it is important for you to understand that these thinking errors are common among everyone—not just people who are depressed. The purpose of learning about them is to learn how to overcome them. It is also important for you to understand that the point of the exercise is not necessarily to be able to identify which thinking error you are engaging in as much as it is for you to recognize that you are making one.*

2. Keep track of the times that you commit such thinking errors over the next three or four days.

3. For each time that you engage in a thinking error, (a) write what you were thinking, (b) write an alternative and more adaptive positive thought, and (c) describe how you would feel if you were to think more positively.

Thinking/thought error: _____

An alternative thought would be: _____

If I were to believe in this alternative thought, I would feel: _____

Thinking/thought error: _____

An alternative thought would be: _____

If I were to believe in this alternative thought, I would feel: _____

# Exercise XII.C

Thinking/thought error: _____

_____

An alternative thought would be: _____

_____

If I was to believe in this alternative thought I would feel: _____

_____

*For fun, see if you can find the thinking errors in the word search below.*

| C | A | T | A | S | T | R | O | P | H | I | Z | I | N | G | B |
|---|---|---|---|---|---|---|---|---|---|---|---|---|---|---|---|
| M | D | F | O | S | R | F | G | H | J | K | B | L | F | B | L |
| I | A | F | V | J | K | L | W | Z | Y | B | J | S | O | J | A |
| N | W | G | R | Y | T | I | T | A | P | Q | G | H | R | K | C |
| D | O | F | R | Q | S | C | G | H | J | K | N | M | T | T | K |
| J | U | D | G | I | N | G | U | H | Q | S | D | D | U | R | W |
| P | M | U | E | E | A | F | J | I | V | S | F | A | N | A | H |
| A | G | G | N | I | Z | I | L | A | N | O | S | R | E | P | I |
| D | G | W | A | K | R | K | O | D | W | V | K | K | T | O | T |
| Q | K | O | R | U | G | Y | N | F | D | E | B | G | E | W | E |
| L | K | U | L | V | S | J | W | N | C | U | O | L | L | N | T |
| Q | W | F | I | L | T | E | R | I | N | G | K | A | L | W | H |
| K | U | H | Z | G | N | I | T | N | U | O | C | S | I | D | I |
| L | C | Z | I | B | T | D | J | N | K | S | V | S | N | N | N |
| K | M | I | N | D | R | E | A | D | I | N | G | E | G | P | K |
| S | Q | G | G | H | E | A | X | C | K | T | D | S | M | L | I |
| S | E | L | F | B | L | A | M | I | N | G | D | F | N | J | N |
| Q | F | S | O | L | B | N | G | K | J | X | G | E | J | K | G |

    Black-white thinking    Discounting    Mind reading

    Catastrophizing    Filtering    Personalizing

    Dark glasses    Fortune-telling    Self-blaming

                             Judging

Therapist's Overview

# THERE'S ALWAYS A SUNRISE

## GOALS OF THE EXERCISE

1. Identify times and situations that you tend to feel happy or positive.
2. Increase skills of self-monitoring and focusing on the positive in life.

## ADDITIONAL HOMEWORK THAT MAY BE APPLICABLE TO DEPRESSION

- Adult Children of Alcoholics  What's My Role?  Page 3
- Anger Control Problems  My Safe Place  Page 33
- Anxiety  Beating Self-Defeating Beliefs  Page 42

## ADDITIONAL PROBLEMS IN WHICH THIS EXERCISE MAY BE USEFUL

- Anxiety
- Anger
- Bulimia and other types of eating disorders

## SUGGESTIONS FOR PROCESSING THIS EXERCISE WITH CLIENT

This exercise is helpful for anyone. It is designed to focus individuals on the positive in their life. The more an individual thinks about and is consciously aware of the positive in their life, the less likely they are to dwell on the negative aspects.

**Exercise XII.D**

# THERE'S ALWAYS A SUNRISE

So much in life is focused on the negative. A simple and probably one of the clearest examples of this is listening to any news broadcast, which tells you about how bad things are in the world. If we constantly think about and focus on the negative aspects in life, we are all bound to be depressed. There is so much more to life than the negative. A major step in overcoming feelings of depression involves focusing on the positive. The following exercise is designed to help you do just that.

Throughout the day think about and record positive thoughts. After one week you will be able to look back on many positives in your life.

1. Each morning when you wake up, and before you get out of bed, tell yourself something positive (e.g., "The sun is shining, it is going to be a beautiful day").
   _____
   _____

2. Before eating your lunch, think about something positive that happened that morning (e.g., "I got a chance to talk with my sister, it was nice to hear from her").
   _____
   _____

3. Before eating dinner, think about something positive that happened that afternoon (e.g., "I made three phone calls to people I needed to speak with. That was something I needed to do and I did it").
   _____
   _____

4. Before going to bed, think of something positive that happened that evening or that happened during the day (e.g., "I was able to think about two positive things today. I am starting to focus on the positive in life more and that makes me feel better about myself").
   _____
   _____

# Section XIII

# DOMESTIC VIOLENCE OFFENDERS

Therapist's Overview

# WHEN DO I NEED A BREAK?

## GOALS OF THE EXERCISE

1. Identify the warning signs of escalation toward violence.
2. Increase self-awareness of the emotional, cognitive, behavioral, and physiological cues.

## ADDITIONAL HOMEWORK THAT MAY BE APPLICABLE TO DOMESTIC VIOLENCE OFFENDERS

- Anger Control Problems — Anger Log — Page 24
- Chemical Dependence — What to Do Instead of Using — Page 82
- Child Sexual Molestation — I'm Changing the Way I Think — Page 100

## ADDITIONAL PROBLEMS IN WHICH THIS EXERCISE MAY BE USEFUL

- Anger Control Problems
- Parenting Problems
- Type-A Stress

## SUGGESTIONS FOR PROCESSING THIS EXERCISE WITH THE CLIENT

Individuals who have engaged in violent behavior toward their partner (or anyone) need to become aware of the warning signs to such behavior. It is often difficult to change this behavior unless one develops the self-monitoring skills to be aware of it when it is occurring. The purpose of the following exercise is to aid individuals in this process.

Exercise XIII.A

# WHEN DO I NEED A BREAK?

The purpose of the following exercise is to help you recognize when you need to take a break.

1. Try to recall the last time you became aggressive and/or violent. Describe the situation and how you reacted.

   _____
   _____
   _____
   _____
   _____
   _____
   _____
   _____

2. In recalling this incident, identify some of the possible warning signs that were present, which indicated that you were escalating.

   What were you feeling physically (e.g., "I felt my chest getting tighter and tighter")?

   _____
   _____
   _____

   What were some of the thoughts that you had (e.g., "This isn't fair," "You _____ ")?

   _____
   _____
   _____

   What were your actions (e.g., "My fists became clenched," "I started pacing")?

   _____
   _____
   _____

Exercise XIII.A

3. Make a list of possible triggers to make you become angry and/or upset and/or violent.

_____
_____
_____
_____
_____
_____
_____
_____

4. Over the next week, keep track of times you started to experience any of the warning signs (physical sensations, thoughts, actions, etc.) that you described earlier.

Day/time: _____

Describe the situation.

_____
_____
_____
_____

Describe the warning signs that you noticed.

_____
_____
_____
_____

Day/time: _____

Describe the situation.

_____
_____
_____
_____

Describe the warning signs that you noticed.

_____
_____
_____
_____

**Therapist's Overview**

# NOW IS WHEN I NEED A BREAK

## GOALS OF THE EXERCISE

1. Identify the warning signs of escalation toward violence.
2. Increase self-awareness of the emotional, cognitive, behavioral, and physiological cues.
3. Develop an agreement between you and your partner regarding taking a time-out.
4. Implement steps toward taking a time-out.

## ADDITIONAL HOMEWORK THAT MAY BE APPLICABLE TO DOMESTIC VIOLENCE OFFENDERS

- Anger Control Problems    Anger Log    Page 24
- Chemical Dependence    What to Do Instead of Using    Page 82
- Child Sexual Molestation    I'm Changing the Way I Think    Page 100

## ADDITIONAL PROBLEMS IN WHICH THIS EXERCISE MAY BE USEFUL

- Anger Control Problems
- Parenting Problems
- Type-A Stress

## SUGGESTIONS FOR PROCESSING THIS EXERCISE WITH THE CLIENT

Use your clinical judgment and supervision to determine whether a session with the couple would be wise. If there is a question of safety for the partner, then have an individual session with the domestic violence offender only. If you determine that a couple's session would be safe, explain how a time-out works. Facilitate a mutual agreement and understanding of what the domestic violence offender will do the next time he/she recognizes the warning signs that his/her behavior is escalating toward violence. The following exercise can be used as a guide to utilizing a time-out.

Exercise XIII.B

# NOW IS WHEN I NEED A BREAK

The following exercise will guide you through the process of using a time-out, in order to calm down and avoid violence. You should be comfortable with, and very aware of, the warning signs (physical sensations, thoughts, and actions), which tend to lead you into violent behavior.

**Step 1.** Whenever you begin to experience any of the warning signs, acknowledge it to yourself (e.g., I am clenching my fist, or my chest is becoming tight. That's a warning that I could become aggressive or violent. Now is when I need to take a break).

**Step 2.** Tell your partner what you are experiencing and that you need a break (e.g., "I am feeling tense and I need to go cool down"). You might want to rate your level of anger on a scale of 1 to 10. The 10 would indicate you are about to explode. Learn to know when you are a 3, so that you can begin to implement the time-out strategy.

**Step 3.** Leave the area and practice relaxation strategies. This could include deep breathing, going for a 5- to 10-minute walk, reading a selected passage that you wrote or that is in a book that helps you calm down, or taking a shower. You will need to identify a list of options that you will use in order to relax and calm down. (See the list that follows.)

**Step 4.** Return to the conversation or situation if you are calm (if your rating is under 4). If you are a 5 or over, this means that you still need a break. If you or others present are not calm, leave the area.

**This is what I can do to calm myself down:**

_____
_____
_____
_____
_____
_____
_____
_____
_____

Therapist's Overview

# I CAN HAVE FEELINGS, TOO

## GOALS OF THE EXERCISE

1. Identify the warning signs of escalation toward violence.
2. Increase self-awareness of the emotional/feeling cues.
3. Learn to feel comfortable with identifying and expressing feelings.

## ADDITIONAL HOMEWORK THAT MAY BE APPLICABLE TO DOMESTIC VIOLENCE OFFENDERS

- Anger Control Problems        Anger Log                          Page 24
- Chemical Dependence           What to Do Instead of Using        Page 82
- Child Sexual Molestation      I'm Changing the Way I Think       Page 100

## ADDITIONAL PROBLEMS IN WHICH THIS EXERCISE MAY BE USEFUL

- Anger Control Problems
- Child Sexual Molestation

## SUGGESTIONS FOR PROCESSING THIS EXERCISE WITH THE CLIENT

This exercise is designed to help individuals identify and express their feelings—all feelings, not just anger and aggression. Prior to assigning this task, discuss the benefits of being aware of one's feelings and being able to express them. Discuss how this aids in being able to meet one's emotional needs. Individuals should also practice using feeling statements. Discuss some of the reasons they do not express their feelings (e.g., "It's not what guys do"), and reinforce the benefits of being able to do so. Individuals also need to complete the homework, "When Do I Need a Break?," prior to being assigned this task.

Exercise XIII.C

# I CAN HAVE FEELINGS, TOO

The purpose of the following exercise is to help you find ways to become aware of the range of feelings that you can experience. You will need to have completed the homework, "When Do I Need a Break?"

1. While reviewing the homework, "When Do I Need a Break?," think about the situation you were describing and identify the feelings you were experiencing. Think about how the situation built up to the point of you becoming violent. Break it down into as many steps as you can and identify the feelings you were experiencing at each step. In the following, record those feelings and what they were a reaction to (e.g., "When she looked at that other guy, I started thinking that she wanted to be with him instead of me. I started to feel jealous and scared that I was going to lose her").

   _____
   _____
   _____
   _____
   _____
   _____
   _____

2. Anytime that you felt angry, think of additional feelings that you were experiencing as well. Remember that anger is a result of physical or emotional pain (e.g., "I was angry and hurt that she was looking at another guy").

3. Make a list of the various feelings you identified in item 1.

   _____        _____
   _____        _____
   _____        _____
   _____        _____

4. Over the next week, keep track of the times you start to experience any of the feelings you listed in item 2.

Exercise XIII.C

5. In a journal, record the feelings by using an "I" statement.

Today I was feeling _____ because _____
_____.

Today I was feeling _____ because _____
_____.

Today I was feeling _____ because _____
_____.

Today I was feeling _____ because _____
_____.

Today I was feeling _____ because _____
_____.

Today I was feeling _____ because _____
_____.

Today I was feeling _____ because _____
_____.

6. In group, read the feelings you experienced and use the "I" statements.

# Section XIV

# DOMESTIC VIOLENCE SURVIVORS

**Therapist's Overview**

# WHAT I GIVE AND WHAT I GET

## GOALS OF THE EXERCISE

1. Increase self-awareness of the emotions and/or feelings related to being in the relationship.
2. Identify the pros and cons of remaining in the relationship.
3. Develop a sense of what kind of relationship you want.

## ADDITIONAL HOMEWORK THAT MAY BE APPLICABLE TO DOMESTIC VIOLENCE SURVIVORS

- Anger Control Problems    My Safe Place                      Page 33
- Anxiety                   Beating Self-Defeating Beliefs     Page 42
- Depression                My Feelings Journal                Page 123
- Rape Survivors            Changing My Faulty Thinking        Page 222
- Rape Survivors            What I Feel and What I Think       Page 225

## ADDITIONAL PROBLEMS IN WHICH THIS EXERCISE MAY BE USEFUL

- Codependence
- Separation and Divorce

## SUGGESTIONS FOR PROCESSING THIS EXERCISE WITH THE CLIENT

Individuals involved in domestic violence need to take a step back from the situation and examine what they like and don't like, as well as what they want and don't want. Unfortunately, these individuals often feel trapped and believe that they have no way out. Before any changes in the relationship can be made, a person must first develop some understanding of what it is they want and don't want. Once they have a better understanding of this, then they can begin to plan ways to achieve what it is they want and deserve. Explain this to the group and that you would like them to describe what they get and give in the relationship. Suggest that they use two pieces of paper, each with a line drawn down the middle. On the first paper, on one side, have them describe what they give, bring, and/or put forth into the relationship and on the other side what they get from the relationship. On the second piece of paper, have them do the same thing, but have them base it on the ideal relationship.

**Exercise XIV.A**

# WHAT I GIVE AND WHAT I GET

If you are in an abusive relationship, you need to identify the pros and cons of staying. One way to do this is by identifying what you put into the relationship and what you get from your partner. No relationship is constantly equal in terms of what you both put into it; however, you need to determine how much you are willing to give and how little you are willing to receive. Finding a way to change the relationship is difficult and is not part of this exercise. One of the first steps to change is recognizing that something needs to be different. The purpose of this exercise is to help you recognize and identify how much you are contributing, how much you are getting back, and what you want in a relationship.

You will need two pieces of paper.

1. Draw a line down the middle of each paper.
2. On the first paper, on one side, describe what you believe you are giving or putting forth into the relationship.
3. On the other side of the page, describe what you get from the relationship. This could be what you get from your partner or from being in the relationship alone (e.g., a place to stay).
4. On the second piece of paper, do the same thing, but this time, base it on what you would consider the ideal relationship.
5. Share this with your group.

Therapist's Overview

# WHAT IF . . . ?

## GOALS OF THE EXERCISE

1. Generate a list of possible outcomes based on staying or leaving.
2. Identify the fears associated with leaving or staying in the abusive relationship.
3. Develop a plan of action to overcome each identified fear.

## ADDITIONAL HOMEWORK THAT MAY BE APPLICABLE TO DOMESTIC VIOLENCE SURVIVORS

| | | |
|---|---|---|
| • Anger Control Problems | My Safe Place | Page 33 |
| • Anxiety | Beating Self-Defeating Beliefs | Page 42 |
| • Depression | My Feelings Journal | Page 123 |
| • Rape Survivors | Changing My Faulty Thinking | Page 222 |
| • Rape Survivors | What I Feel and What I Think | Page 225 |

## ADDITIONAL PROBLEMS IN WHICH THIS EXERCISE MAY BE USEFUL

- Codependence
- Separation and Divorce

## SUGGESTIONS FOR PROCESSING THIS EXERCISE WITH THE CLIENT

The purpose of this exercise is to help individuals who are in an abusive relationship to generate some of the pros and cons to remaining or leaving. A concern to address with the group is what if an abusive partner finds this homework, how will he/she react? Steps should be taken to keep private any material that could incite the partner and lead to more abuse.

Exercise XIV.B

# WHAT IF . . . ?

This exercise is designed to help you evaluate the pros and cons of remaining or leaving your current situation. You will be able to put in writing your fears to either decision and generate a list of what you could do to overcome each fear.

1. Describe a good day or time with your partner.

   _____
   _____
   _____
   _____
   _____

2. Describe a bad day or time with your partner.

   _____
   _____
   _____
   _____
   _____

3. List the positive qualities that you see in your partner.

   _____
   _____
   _____
   _____

4. List the negative qualities that you see in your partner.

   _____
   _____
   _____
   _____
   _____

Exercise XIV.B

5. Describe what you think it would be like to live away from your partner or on your own. Be sure to include your thoughts regarding finances, social life, emotional support, friendships, family life, effect on children, and anything else you think of.

___

6. Go back to item 5 and highlight any fears you identified if you were to leave.
7. Describe why you think each fear is likely or unlikely to become a reality.

___

8. Describe at least two ways that you would deal with each fear.

___

Therapist's Overview

# THOUGHTS ABOUT THIS RELATIONSHIP

## GOALS OF THE EXERCISE

1. Challenge minimization of abusive relationship.
2. Challenge self-blame for violence.
3. Generate more positive and self-affirming beliefs.
4. Encourage group support and greater cohesion.

## ADDITIONAL HOMEWORK THAT MAY BE APPLICABLE TO DOMESTIC VIOLENCE SURVIVORS

- Anger Control Problems    My Safe Place                      Page 33
- Anxiety                   Beating Self-Defeating Beliefs     Page 42
- Depression                My Feelings Journal                Page 123
- Rape Survivors            Changing My Faulty Thinking        Page 222
- Rape Survivors            What I Feel and What I Think       Page 225

## ADDITIONAL PROBLEMS IN WHICH THIS EXERCISE MAY BE USEFUL

- Codependence
- Separation and Divorce

## SUGGESTIONS FOR PROCESSING THIS EXERCISE WITH THE CLIENT

This exercise is a homework assignment for the whole group. There are three phases involved. The first phase involves each member writing a letter, which describes their thoughts regarding their tolerance or acceptance of the abuse within the relationship. Tell the group that you would like them to bring in their letters at the next group meeting. Explain that at that time they will be sharing their letters with each other. At the next group meeting, have each member exchange letters with one other group member. Explain that at this point, you would like them to review the letter they received and identify any distorted or self-critical type of thinking (e.g., minimizing of the abuse, blaming self for the abuse instead of holding the partner responsible for his/her violent behavior). Once this is complete, each member is to rewrite the letter they reviewed, omitting any distorted thinking and replacing it with more assertive talk. The purpose of this exercise is to empower each member to recognize his/her minimizations and rationalizations regarding the abuse. It is also helpful in creating greater support and cohesiveness within the group.

Exercise XIV.C

# THOUGHTS ABOUT THIS RELATIONSHIP

Write a letter describing how you manage to deal with or tolerate the violence or threat of violence within your relationship. Describe some of the altercations you have experienced and any reasons or explanations you have formulated in your own mind to make sense of why they happen. Bring this letter to your next group session. Each group member will be asked to share theirs with the group.

# Section XV

# GRIEF/LOSS UNRESOLVED

Therapist's Overview

# FAREWELL, UNTIL WE MEET AGAIN

## GOALS OF THE EXERCISE

1. Begin the process of letting go and moving on.
2. Identify your feelings regarding the one you lost.

## ADDITIONAL HOMEWORK THAT MAY BE APPLICABLE TO GRIEF/LOSS UNRESOLVED

- Depression           My Feelings Journal         Page 123
- Incest Survivors—Adult     What I Need to Tell You     Page 179

## ADDITIONAL PROBLEMS IN WHICH THIS EXERCISE MAY BE USEFUL

- Adult Children of Alcoholics
- Separation and Divorce

## SUGGESTIONS FOR PROCESSING THIS EXERCISE WITH THE CLIENT

Encourage the group to write a letter of farewell to the person whom they've lost. In group, discuss some of the times and qualities they remember about the person who passed away. Have them use this discussion to aid in writing the letter.

Exercise XV.A

# FAREWELL, UNTIL WE MEET AGAIN

This exercise is designed to help you write a letter of farewell to the person who has passed away. You may want to review photo albums or just think back about the times you spent with that person. Try to think about the feelings you have now as well as those you felt when you were with that person.

1. Think about the various times that you were with the person who passed away. Try to remember times when you had fun together, when you were angry at him/her or he/she was angry with you, a reason you admired or did not admire him/her, a time you were worried about him/her, and any other time that comes to mind.

2. Describe your favorite story of the person who passed away.

   _____
   _____
   _____
   _____
   _____

3. Describe the last time that you were with _____ (person who passed away). Write and/or draw the feelings you experienced.

   _____
   _____
   _____
   _____
   _____

4. Describe any thoughts and feelings that you had but did not share with the person who passed away.

   _____
   _____
   _____
   _____
   _____

Exercise XV.A

5. Describe what _____ died from.

_____
_____
_____
_____

6. Write, draw, or use a picture to describe how you heard the news. Where were you and who told you?

_____
_____
_____
_____

7. Write, draw, or use a picture to describe what you remember thinking and feeling when you found out.

_____
_____
_____
_____

8. Write, draw, or use a picture to describe the service and/or funeral.

_____
_____
_____
_____

9. Write, draw, or use a picture to describe three positive memories and/or images that you will never forget.

_____
_____
_____
_____

10. Share your letter or album that you have just created with the group and anyone else with whom you feel comfortable in doing so.

Therapist's Overview

# MOVING ON

## GOALS OF THE EXERCISE

1. Begin the process of letting go and moving on.
2. Develop a conceptualization of how things would be in your life once you moved on.
3. Implement a plan of creating how you would want things to be to indicate that you have been able to move on with your life.

## ADDITIONAL HOMEWORK THAT MAY BE APPLICABLE TO GRIEF/LOSS UNRESOLVED

- Depression     My Feelings Journal     Page 123
- Incest Survivors—Adult     What I Need to Tell You     Page 179

## ADDITIONAL PROBLEMS IN WHICH THIS EXERCISE MAY BE USEFUL

- Separation and Divorce

## SUGGESTIONS FOR PROCESSING THIS EXERCISE WITH THE CLIENT

Loss and grief are also experienced when we change jobs, move, or become separated or divorced. It is important for any individual who is experiencing a loss, whether it be the loss of a loved one or the loss of a career, home, or something else, that he or she be able to pick up the pieces and move on. This exercise is designed to help such individuals identify what life would look like if they in fact were able to pick up the pieces and move on. It is important to identify the feelings that are associated with any loss, and it is also important to foster a grieving process. However, individuals also need to develop the coping skills and plans of how to overcome and get past their grief. Use your clinical judgment in deciding when the individuals in your group are ready to move on. Be sure that they have had the opportunity and the forum in which to experience their loss and express the associated thoughts and feelings.

Exercise XV.B

# MOVING ON

This exercise is designed to help you identify ways to pick up the pieces after experiencing a loss of any kind and to develop a plan of how you will move on. It will also aid you in putting such a plan into practice.

1. It is important for you to have identified and expressed any hurt and sadness you have experienced as a result of your loss. Try to identify the thoughts that come to mind regarding the following feelings.

    I am angry because _____
    _____
    _____ .

    I am saddened because _____
    _____
    _____ .

    I will miss _____
    _____
    _____ .

    I am thankful that _____
    _____
    _____ .

    Use the remaining lines to describe any other thoughts and feelings regarding your loss.

    _____
    _____
    _____
    _____
    _____

2. Describe how things were before this loss. First, describe what you liked about your situation.

___

Describe what you did not like about your situation.

___

3. Describe how you would like things to be in your life now. What would you wish for?

___

4. Right now, you may not feel like you are where you want to be regarding your well-being—emotionally, physically, financially, and so on. Try to conceptualize and describe how things would be if you were feeling that everything was how it should be and that you have moved on. Basically, finish the following statement for all aspects of your life (e.g., emotionally, physically, socially, financially, family life, etc.): I will know that I have moved on and that I am feeling stable (emotionally, physically, socially, financially, family life, etc.) when

___

5. Break this last answer down into steps to be completed. For example, "I will know that I have moved on and that I am feeling emotionally stable when I am rating my daily life as positive 80 percent of the time. Or when I am no longer crying on a daily basis. Or when I am feeling calmer and relaxed because I have not yelled, cried, and so on for over two weeks. I will know that I have moved on and that I am feeling physically stable when I have gained 10 pounds and kept it on for over two weeks. I will know that I have moved on and that I am feeling financially stable when I have been able to put away and save 10 percent of my paycheck for at least five pay periods."

It may also be helpful to put time frames or target dates as to when you plan to be meeting your goal: "By the beginning of next month I will have saved $_____. Or by the beginning of next month I will be exercising at least two times a week." Use the following lines to describe your plan of how you will know that you have moved on.

_____
_____
_____
_____
_____
_____
_____
_____
_____
_____
_____
_____
_____
_____

# Section XVI

# HIV/AIDS

Therapist's Overview

# HOW AM I DOING?

## GOALS OF THE EXERCISE

1. Honestly evaluate your current view of your situation.
2. Identify the associated feelings and thoughts.

## ADDITIONAL HOMEWORK THAT MAY BE APPLICABLE TO HIV/AIDS

- Depression             My Feelings Journal              Page 123
- Grief/Loss Unresolved  Farewell, until We Meet Again    Page 150

## ADDITIONAL PROBLEMS IN WHICH THIS EXERCISE MAY BE USEFUL

- Depression
- Grief/Loss Unresolved

## SUGGESTIONS FOR PROCESSING THIS EXERCISE WITH THE CLIENT

This exercise is designed to help individuals take stock of their current situation. Let them know that it is helpful to identify the thoughts and feelings regarding how they are managing. This is also helpful for you as a clinician to assess their levels of depression, anxiety, and so forth. Explain that this homework is a check-in. You want to check in with them regarding how they are perceiving their current status, as well as how they are coping with it. This exercise is also helpful to you in gaining basic information about each person's condition.

Exercise XVI.A

# HOW AM I DOING?

This exercise is for you to evaluate your thoughts and feelings regarding your view of your current situation and how you are managing. Try to be as open and as honest with yourself as you can. This exercise is also helpful for your therapist because it will give him/her some insight regarding your perceptions and style of coping.

1. Briefly describe and list your current medical conditions and diagnosis.

   _____
   _____
   _____
   _____
   _____
   _____
   _____
   _____

2. List each medication you are currently being prescribed and what it is for.

   _____
   _____
   _____
   _____
   _____

3. Briefly describe the course of your condition to date.

   _____
   _____
   _____
   _____
   _____
   _____
   _____
   _____

Exercise XVI.A

4. In describing the preceding information, identify the associated thoughts and feelings you are experiencing and have experienced.

   _____
   _____
   _____
   _____
   _____
   _____
   _____
   _____

5. What do you view as the worst aspect of your condition and why?

   _____
   _____
   _____
   _____
   _____
   _____
   _____
   _____

6. On a scale of 1 to 10, 1 representing not managing well at all and 10 meaning that you have it all under control, rate how you feel you are handling things.

7. Describe why you rated item 6 the way you did.

   _____
   _____
   _____
   _____

8. Describe how things would be in order for you to rate how you are handling things as a 10.

   _____
   _____
   _____
   _____
   _____

Therapist's Overview

# WHY ME?

## GOALS OF THE EXERCISE

1. Honestly evaluate your current view of your situation.
2. Identify the associated feelings and thoughts.
3. Evaluate behavior for level of continued risk.
4. Identify and challenge any distorted thinking.

## ADDITIONAL HOMEWORK THAT MAY BE APPLICABLE TO HIV/AIDS

- Anxiety                  Beating Self-Defeating Beliefs     Page 42
- Depression               My Feelings Journal                Page 123
- Grief/Loss Unresolved    Farewell, until We Meet Again      Page 150

## ADDITIONAL PROBLEMS IN WHICH THIS EXERCISE MAY BE USEFUL

- Depression
- Grief/Loss Unresolved

## SUGGESTIONS FOR PROCESSING THIS EXERCISE WITH THE CLIENT

This exercise will help individuals talk about how they view themselves and their current situation. Explore with them what are high-risk behaviors and what are cognitive distortions. Give each individual a list of cognitive distortions. (For a list of cognitive distortions, see "Taking Charge of Your Thoughts," in Section XII, "Depression.") This exercise is helpful for you, as well as your clients, to take a step back and evaluate what they are doing to stay emotionally and physically healthy.

Exercise XVI.B

# WHY ME?

This exercise is designed to help you to take a step back and evaluate what and how you are managing to stay emotionally and physically healthy. You will be asked to evaluate your view of yourself, your current behaviors, and thoughts. High-risk behaviors and negative thinking (cognitive distortions) will be identified and challenged.

1. The title of this exercise is called "Why Me?" Try to answer that question in regard to your current medical, physical, and emotional condition.

   _____
   _____
   _____
   _____
   _____
   _____

2. Review the list of cognitive distortions. Check to see which ones you tend to engage in and record several examples.

   _____
   _____
   _____
   _____
   _____

3. For each distortion that you gave an example of, write two alternative and more positive self-affirming statements. (If you are struggling, ask someone to whom you are close and who cares about you to help.)

   _____
   _____
   _____
   _____
   _____
   _____
   _____

Exercise XVI.B

4. Reread your response to item 1.

5. Try to identify what behaviors you had, as well as those you continue to engage in, that are considered high-risk.

6. Describe your reasons for continuing to engage in these high-risk behaviors. (If you have discontinued all high-risk behaviors, describe what your reasons were for engaging in them when you did.)

7. Identify the cognitive distortions you used to make it okay for you to engage in such high-risk behaviors.

8. Record statements that you can use (have used) to counter such negative thinking.

Exercise XVI.B

9. In what other activities can you engage, instead of the high-risk ones that you have identified?

10. Explain why you should avoid the high-risk behaviors previously described.

11. Describe any reason(s) you can think of to support an argument for continuing to engage in any of the high-risk behaviors or cognitive distortions you described in this exercise.

12. Share the responses to this exercise with the rest of your group members.

# Section XVII

# INCEST OFFENDERS—ADULT

Therapist's Overview

# THROUGH THE EYES OF A CHILD

## GOALS OF THE EXERCISE

1. Identify the various thoughts, feelings, and reactions your victim experienced during and after the sexual abuse.
2. Begin to develop an understanding of the emotional, physical, social, and developmental difficulties experienced by victims.

## ADDITIONAL HOMEWORK THAT MAY BE APPLICABLE TO INCEST OFFENDERS

- Child Sexual Molestation — This Is What Happened — Page 93
- Child Sexual Molestation — This Is What I Did — Page 96
- Child Sexual Molestation — I'm Changing the Way I Think — Page 100
- Child Sexual Molestation — Stop! Rewind! And Start Again — Page 103

## ADDITIONAL PROBLEMS IN WHICH THIS EXERCISE MAY BE USEFUL

- Child Sexual Molestation

## SUGGESTIONS FOR PROCESSING THIS EXERCISE WITH THE CLIENT

Individuals who have offended often view what they did from their own point of view. This exercise requires them to see and get a sense of what a victim experiences. Before assigning this, individuals should be able to explain in detail the stages and progression of the abuse. If possible, individuals should be provided with excerpts from victims regarding the effects they experienced.

Exercise XVII.A

# THROUGH THE EYES OF A CHILD

This exercise is geared to help you develop a greater perspective of the effects of the sexual abuse from the standpoint of your victim. You will need to be able to describe what you did, including how you groomed your victim, how the physical acts of sexual abuse occurred and progressed, as well as how the situation stands currently.

1. Describe the different ways that you groomed your victim.

2. How old was he/she when this started?

3. What was a typical day like for him/her (or a child at that age)?

4. What might he/she have been thinking and feeling during the times that you were grooming him/her?

5. Describe how you began to sexually abuse your victim in a physical way (e.g., fondling).

Exercise XVII.A

6. What might your victim have been thinking and feeling when you were doing these things?

   _____
   _____
   _____
   _____

7. During these situations, how did you end it? Did you tell him/her to go get dressed? Did you not say anything and just leave? How did he/she know it was over?

   _____
   _____
   _____
   _____

8. What might your victim have been thinking and feeling when it was over?

   _____
   _____
   _____
   _____

9. Imagine being your victim. Imagine as your victim that you have just been sexually assaulted by you. Imagine meeting up with your brother or sister or other parent. What might you (as your victim) be thinking and feeling?

   _____
   _____
   _____
   _____

10. Imagine the same scenario as described in item 9, but this time you are meeting up with your friends. What thoughts and feelings might you be having if you were your victim and you were just sexually assaulted by you?

    _____
    _____
    _____
    _____

11. Imagine going to bed at night and thinking about having been sexually assaulted by you. As your victim, how might you be thinking and feeling?

    _____
    _____
    _____
    _____

Exercise XVII.A

12. Describe at last three other situations in which you imagine being your victim. Describe the situation and what your victim may be thinking and feeling.

   _____

13. How did the abuse stop? Did your victim tell? Did someone find out indirectly? Describe how it was disclosed.

   _____

14. Describe how your victim might be thinking and feeling about how you have been treating him/her.

   _____

15. What is your relationship to your victim (e.g., father)?
   _____

16. What might your victim be thinking and feeling about you as his/her (e.g., father)?

   _____

17. As your victim, how might he/she be thinking and feeling about himself/herself?

   _____

Therapist's Overview

# STRESS AND TRIGGER JOURNAL

## GOALS OF THE EXERCISE

1. Identify the various thoughts and feelings you experience throughout each day, which may lead to stress and serve as a possible trigger to relapse.
2. Begin to develop an understanding of the thinking errors or cognitive distortions you use, which contribute to putting you at risk for relapse.
3. Begin to develop an understanding of the thinking errors or cognitive distortions you used to convince yourself that the sexual offending was okay.

## ADDITIONAL HOMEWORK THAT MAY BE APPLICABLE TO INCEST OFFENDERS

- Child Sexual Molestation   This Is What Happened          Page 93
- Child Sexual Molestation   This Is What I Did             Page 96
- Child Sexual Molestation   I'm Changing the Way I Think   Page 100
- Child Sexual Molestation   Stop! Rewind! And Start Again  Page 103

## ADDITIONAL PROBLEMS IN WHICH THIS EXERCISE MAY BE USEFUL

- Child Sexual Molestation
- Domestic Violence Offender

## SUGGESTIONS FOR PROCESSING THIS EXERCISE WITH CLIENT

This exercise is designed to help individuals become familiar with their typical daily thoughts, feelings, and reactions to their daily life experiences. This exercise will help individuals increase their ability to self-monitor. It would be good for you to review with your group members the various types of cognitive distortions and give multiple examples of each. For a list of cognitive distortions, see "What Am I Thinking?" under Section VI, "Bulimia," of this book.

Exercise XVII.B

# STRESS AND TRIGGER JOURNAL

This exercise is designed to help you become more familiar with your daily thoughts, feelings, and reactions to your daily life experiences. It will help you to identify any thinking errors or cognitive distortions in which you engage. Once you are able to identify such distortions, you have more control over being able to redirect your thoughts as well as your behavior. In doing so, you will be able to reduce your risk of reoffending greatly.

You will need any kind of notebook and some time each day to record your thoughts, feelings, and reactions. In trying to think about what to write, try to focus on times throughout the day that you felt stressed, rejected and/or ignored, as well as excited. Be sure to include times that you engaged in any sexual fantasies.

It is sometimes helpful to have a regularly scheduled time in which you write in your journal (e.g., just before going to sleep). Other people prefer to write in their journal throughout the day so that what they record is fresher in their mind and generally more accurate. You will need to decide which works best for you.

Be sure that you are familiar with the various types of thinking errors or cognitive distortions. You may want to ask your therapist for a list of different cognitive distortions, so that you can review it at home.

One other idea is to generate a list of situations that you know makes you stressed, feel rejected and/or ignored, angry, as well as excited. By creating a list, you become more consciously aware of such times. This will not only help you with your journal writing, but it will help you stay more in control of your reactions.

For each day that you write in your journal, be sure to include the following information:

- Date and time that you were writing
- Feelings that you experienced
- Thoughts that went through your mind (including any sexual fantasies)
- Whether any of these thoughts were thinking errors or cognitive distortions
- How you redirected your distortions
- How you redirected your reactions and/or behavior

After you have written in your journal for the day, reread what you wrote. Ask yourself how what you wrote might apply to when you were offending your victim. For example, "Did I use those distortions to convince myself that what I was doing was okay?"

**Therapist's Overview**

# MY LETTER OF APOLOGY

## GOALS OF THE EXERCISE

1. Demonstrate full responsibility for your offending behavior.
2. Explain what you did was wrong and why.
3. Express remorse for what you did.

## ADDITIONAL HOMEWORK THAT MAY BE APPLICABLE TO INCEST OFFENDERS

- Child Sexual Molestation    This Is What Happened           Page 93
- Child Sexual Molestation    This Is What I Did              Page 96
- Child Sexual Molestation    I'm Changing the Way I Think    Page 100
- Child Sexual Molestation    Stop! Rewind! And Start Again   Page 103

## ADDITIONAL PROBLEMS IN WHICH THIS EXERCISE MAY BE USEFUL

- Child Sexual Molestation
- Domestic Violence Offender

## SUGGESTIONS FOR PROCESSING THIS EXERCISE WITH THE CLIENT

This exercise should only be used with individuals who have shown a positive attitude toward treatment and have been able to utilize treatment effectively. This would include group members who have been able to take full responsibility of their offending behavior, are aware of their offending cycle (e.g., triggers and subsequent thoughts and behaviors), are able to verbalize and put into practice strategies to redirect and/or avoid situations that could lead them to reoffend, and who have been able to shown signs of empathy.

Exercise XVII.C

# MY LETTER OF APOLOGY

In writing a letter of apology, you must keep several guidelines in mind.

- Use "I" statements.
- Explain what you did in general terms (e.g., "when I took advantage of you," or "when I manipulated you into doing things you didn't want to do," versus "when I made you touch my penis"). Do not be graphic.
- Describe why what you did was wrong.
- Do not ask for forgiveness. Only explain and state that you are sorry.
- You can describe your progress in treatment and what you have learned.

# Section XVIII

# INCEST SURVIVORS—ADULT

Therapist's Overview

# MY STORY

## GOALS OF THE EXERCISE

1. Be able to describe what happened and the accompanying thoughts and feelings.
2. Develop a sense of empowerment by describing yourself as a survivor.

## ADDITIONAL HOMEWORK THAT MAY BE APPLICABLE TO INCEST SURVIVORS

| | | |
|---|---|---|
| • Domestic Violence Survivors | What If . . . ? | Page 144 |
| • Rape Survivors | Changing My Faulty Thinking | Page 222 |

## ADDITIONAL PROBLEMS IN WHICH THIS EXERCISE MAY BE USEFUL

- Domestic Violence Survivors
- Rape Survivors

## SUGGESTIONS FOR PROCESSING THIS EXERCISE WITH THE CLIENT

This exercise is for individuals to have a chance to describe their story and to be heard and acknowledged. Explain to the group that each person will have an opportunity to describe what happened to him/her.

Exercise XVIII.A

# MY STORY

This exercise will provide you with some basic questions and sentence prompts to help you tell what happened. The purpose is for you to be able to verbalize what happened versus keeping it inside. You will also be encouraged to describe a new ending or an ending that has yet to develop. This ending will provide you with one way of learning how to be a survivor instead of a victim.

1. How old were you when the abuse started?
   _____

2. Who was the person (people) who offended you?
   _____

3. How old was he/she?
   _____

4. Where did the abuse happen?
   _____

5. Describe the location in as much detail as possible (e.g., color of the room, number of windows, furniture, etc.).
   _____
   _____
   _____

6. What time of day would the abuse usually occur?
   _____

7. Who else was around and/or where was the rest of your family members?
   _____

8. If the abuse occurred more than once, describe how you knew when it was going to happen. In other words, what cues did you learn to read that would tell you it was going to happen again?
   _____
   _____
   _____

Exercise XVIII.A

9. Describe what happened.

   What did _____ (person who offended you) say first?
   _____

   How did (person who offended you) touch you and/or have you touch him/her?
   _____
   _____
   _____

   How did you know when it was over?
   _____
   _____
   _____

   What would _____ (person who offended you) say to you?
   _____

10. Did you keep what happened to you a secret?
    _____

11. How long did you keep it to yourself?
    _____

12. What were some of the things that you were afraid of happening if you told?
    _____
    _____
    _____

13. How were those fears reinforced? Did the person who offended you threaten you in any way?
    _____
    _____
    _____

14. What were some of your thoughts and feelings regarding the other members of your family?
    _____
    _____
    _____

15. How did other people finally find out?
    _____
    _____
    _____

Exercise XVIII.A

16. How did your family react (say or do) when they found out?

17. What were some of your thoughts and feelings when the abuse was discovered?

18. What happened after the abuse was discovered?

19. The worst part of the abuse was

20. My thoughts and feelings about _____ (person who offended you) are

21. What I wish most is

22. I am a survivor because

23. My plans for my future, as well as currently, include

Therapist's Overview

# WHAT I NEED TO TELL YOU

## GOALS OF THE EXERCISE

1. Be able to describe your thoughts and feelings regarding others in your life while you were being abused, as well as now.
2. Develop a sense of empowerment by being able to verbalize the various thoughts and feelings that you have held inside and have not been able to express.
3. Begin to create some sense of closure regarding your thoughts and feelings toward significant individuals in your life.

## ADDITIONAL HOMEWORK THAT MAY BE APPLICABLE TO INCEST SURVIVORS

- Caregiver Burnout    This Is for Me and That's Okay         Page 71
- Depression           What Do Others Value about Me?         Page 121
- Depression           My Feelings Journal                    Page 123

## ADDITIONAL PROBLEMS IN WHICH THIS EXERCISE MAY BE USEFUL

- Grief/Loss Unresolved

## SUGGESTIONS FOR PROCESSING THIS EXERCISE WITH THE CLIENT

This assignment is to aid individuals in being able to express the thoughts and feelings they have regarding various people in their life but have been unable to give voice to such thoughts and feelings. An example of how this assignment can be used is for individuals who need to be able to express their anger or forgiveness to the parent who was unable to protect them. Another example is for the individual who needs to be able to tell his or her perpetrator that he/she has survived and will no longer be controlled by the abuse. This assignment would be helpful for any individual who needs to be able to express feelings and thoughts to people they cannot talk to directly, for whatever reason. Instruct group members to think of people whom they need or want to say something to but can't (e.g., person has died, no contact is allowed, etc.). Have them discuss their feelings about these individuals in group. As a homework, have individuals write a letter to the people they identified and bring this letter in to the next session.

**Exercise XVIII.B**

# WHAT I NEED TO TELL YOU

This exercise is for you to be able to put in writing the thoughts and feelings you have kept inside but have not been able to say to those individuals who have affected you throughout your life. The purpose is to help you create some closure and give your thoughts and feelings a voice. You may want to tell the person who offended you a few things but can't for whatever reason. You may want to tell a parent that you are angry with them for not protecting you but you have now reached a point in your life that you can forgive them. Whatever your thoughts and feelings are, they are valid and you deserve to express them. What you do with your writing is ultimately up to you. For example, some people tear up the letter after they have written it and read it aloud. Throwing away the pieces represents throwing away or getting rid of those feelings and/or thoughts. It is recommended that you review your letter with your therapist and your group members.

1. Think of those people in your life to whom you need to say something and list them.

   _____          _____

   _____          _____

   _____          _____

   _____          _____

2. Pick one of these individuals and imagine being able to say whatever comes to your mind.
3. If this is worrisome, imagine that these individuals cannot say or do anything in retaliation, unless you direct it. You can imagine being a writer or director of a movie or a play—what you say goes.
4. You may also want to imagine sheets of Plexiglas™ (how many sheets is up to you), which will protect you from any harm.
5. You may also want to write the type of response you would want from the individual(s) to whom you are speaking. Discuss the pros and cons of doing this with your therapist. You may also want to role-play this scenario in a group session. You be you and then pick a person to be whomever it is you are writing to. You describe how you want the other person to respond.

# Section XIX

# INFERTILITY

Therapist's Overview

# BEING A PARENT MEANS . . .

## GOALS OF THE EXERCISE

1. Be able to express your thoughts and feelings regarding your hopes to be a parent or your thoughts and feelings if you cannot be a biological parent.
2. Be able to identify the thoughts and feelings you have toward your partner.
3. Be able to identify any cognitive distortions and learn to redirect and replace such negative thinking.

## ADDITIONAL HOMEWORK THAT MAY BE APPLICABLE TO INFERTILITY

- Caregiver Burnout       What Drawer Does This Belong In?        Page 74
- Depression              My Feelings Journal                     Page 123

## ADDITIONAL PROBLEMS IN WHICH THIS EXERCISE MAY BE USEFUL

- Grief/Loss Unresolved

## SUGGESTIONS FOR PROCESSING THIS EXERCISE WITH THE CLIENT

Individuals experiencing difficulty conceiving children or who have been told that they are unable to conceive experience a range of emotions, as you can imagine. These feelings can be directed toward themselves, as well as their partner. This exercise will help them to focus on such thoughts and feelings. It will also bring their attention to any thinking errors or distortions in which they are engaging and to develop some ways for them to redirect and replace such negative thinking. It would be beneficial if you could provide group members with a list of cognitive distortions. (See "Taking Charge of Your Thoughts" in Section XII, "Depression.") Explain to the group that all feelings are valid, and encourage them to identify the range of emotions that they are experiencing. It will also be important for group members to discuss this exercise with their spouse or partner.

Exercise XIX.A

# BEING A PARENT MEANS...

This exercise will help you put some of your thoughts and feelings into perspective. Many of the questions and sentence stems you will be reading will probably be things that you have thought about. You will achieve at least three benefits from completing this exercise. First, it will help you to be able to externalize your thoughts and feelings by writing them down. Second, it can provide some guidance in being able to talk with your partner or spouse about your thoughts and feelings. A third benefit is for you to identify any thinking errors (cognitive distortions) as well as ways to redirect such negative thinking.

1. I want to be a parent because _____

2. When I think of not being able to give birth to my children, I think

3. The feelings that I experience when I think of not being able to have my own biological children are

4. What thoughts and feelings do you have regarding your spouse?

Exercise XIX.A

5. What thoughts and feelings do you have regarding yourself?

6. What thoughts and feelings have you not discussed with your spouse?

7. What keeps you from sharing these thoughts and feelings?

8. Review the list of cognitive distortions provided by your therapist. Try to identify in which thinking errors you tend to engage, and write down some examples.

9. For each thinking error (cognitive distortion) you listed in item 8, write an alternative thought, which would serve to counter or negate the negative thought.

10. In thinking about how you would like or need your partner to respond to you in order to discuss these thoughts and feelings, try to describe a scenario in which he or she is able to listen and understand your thoughts and feelings.

11. Review this exercise with your group and practice role-playing how you would discuss your thoughts and feelings with your partner or spouse. Explain to your role-play partner what you would need him/her to do, so that you would feel heard and understood.

Therapist's Overview

# WHAT IF WE HAVE A CHILD SOME OTHER WAY?

## GOALS OF THE EXERCISE

1. Be able to express your thoughts and feelings, especially the fears of alternative treatment options to conceiving or having a child (e.g., artificial insemination with unknown sperm donor, surrogate mother, or adoption).
2. Be able to identify your own emotional needs in making this decision.
3. Learn to find ways to have your emotional needs met.

## ADDITIONAL HOMEWORK THAT MAY BE APPLICABLE TO INFERTILITY

- Caregiver Burnout      What Drawer Does This Belong In?      Page 74
- Depression             My Feelings Journal                   Page 123

## ADDITIONAL PROBLEMS IN WHICH THIS EXERCISE MAY BE USEFUL

- Caregiver Burnout

## SUGGESTIONS FOR PROCESSING THIS EXERCISE WITH THE CLIENT

This exercise can be useful if you are helping group members identify and process the various factors involved in deciding to pursue different treatment options to having a child. Utilize the natural advantage of a group to brainstorm what the different options are and what each person knows about them. Once people have more information on the options available, suggest the following exercise to help them express their thoughts and feelings, especially their fears, regarding these options.

Exercise XIX.B

# WHAT IF WE HAVE A CHILD SOME OTHER WAY?

Becoming aware of the various options available to having a child and then trying to make a decision as to which option to pursue can easily overwhelm you. The decision you choose is obviously a difficult one; however, sometimes what makes it more difficult is keeping your thoughts and feelings inside. One way to decrease the stress of feeling overwhelmed is by putting your thoughts and feelings down on paper. This allows you to externalize them and in some way take some of the weight off, so to speak. The following exercise will help you to focus on the treatment options you are leaning toward pursuing. You will have the chance to identify the pros and cons as well as your thoughts and feelings.

1. List the top three options you are leaning toward pursuing (e.g., artificial insemination with an unknown sperm donor, surrogate mother, or adoption).
   _____
   _____

2. List your fears regarding choosing each one of these options (e.g., Will I be able to love this child? Can we afford the medical costs?).
   _____
   _____

3. List the pros and cons for each option.

   Option 1: _____

   | Pros | Cons |
   | --- | --- |
   |  |  |
   |  |  |
   |  |  |
   |  |  |
   |  |  |

Exercise XIX.B

Option 2: _____

| Pros | Cons |
|------|------|
| _____ | _____ |
| _____ | _____ |
| _____ | _____ |
| _____ | _____ |
| _____ | _____ |
| _____ | _____ |
| _____ | _____ |

Option 3: _____

| Pros | Cons |
|------|------|
| _____ | _____ |
| _____ | _____ |
| _____ | _____ |
| _____ | _____ |
| _____ | _____ |
| _____ | _____ |
| _____ | _____ |

4. How has this decision process been affecting your relationship with your spouse or partner?

5. How has this process been affecting you (emotionally, physically, at work, with friends, with family members, etc.)?

Exercise XIX.B

6. What would ease your mind or make you feel less stressed?

7. List the people in your life who make up your support system.

8. Describe how you have been utilizing your support system or why you have not.

9. If you have not done so in item 6, describe at least three self-nurturing activities that would help you in meeting your emotional needs.

10. Describe a date and time when you will plan on engaging in at least one of the self-nurturing activities you described in item 9.

11. Repeat the directions in item 10 at least once a week.

# Section XX

# PARENTING PROBLEMS

Therapist's Overview

# WORKING FROM THE SAME PAGE

## GOALS OF THE EXERCISE

1. Both parents to be able to identify their expectations of their children, themselves, and each other regarding family life.
2. Each parent to be able to identify and express his/her thoughts and feelings regarding what is okay and not okay behavior.
3. Parents to find support from each other in their approach to parenting.
4. Parents decrease the amount of conflict between themselves regarding parenting issues.

## ADDITIONAL HOMEWORK THAT MAY BE APPLICABLE TO PARENTING PROBLEMS

- Anger Control Problems   Go Blow Out Some Candles   Page 31
- Caregiver Burnout   What Drawer Does This Belong In?   Page 74
- Separation and Divorce   We Need to Agree   Page 231

## ADDITIONAL PROBLEMS IN WHICH THIS EXERCISE MAY BE USEFUL

- Separation and Divorce

## SUGGESTIONS FOR PROCESSING THIS EXERCISE WITH THE CLIENT

Explain to the group how parenting problems often can stem from parents having different expectations and different approaches to dealing with their children. Frequently, when parents are on different pages, the mixed messages that they send create and reinforce the oppositional behavior they see in their children. Describe to the group that in order for families to improve their relationships and decrease conflicts, one step must be for parents to get on the same page with regard to expectations of their children, each other, and themselves. The following exercise is designed to give parents an opportunity to describe what they want in their family life, as well as what they are willing to give or put into it.

Exercise XX.A

# WORKING FROM THE SAME PAGE

Parenting is the most difficult job in the world. You never have a day off. There are no pay raises. Life as you knew it was never the same once you had a child. As fellow parents you know exactly what I am talking about. So how can parents survive being parents? One key to survival and fulfillment as a parent is the luxury of being coparents. To be coparents, however, is not as easy as it may sound. Getting on the same page in order to have children wasn't so hard. Staying on the same page and recognizing what the page looks like once children are born is a whole other story. The following exercise is designed to guide you in the direction of becoming or strengthening your unity as coparents. Each spouse should complete the following:

1. List the top five concerns that you have regarding dealing with the children.

   _____
   _____
   _____
   _____

2. List the various ways you attempt to redirect or parent your children (e.g., time-out, no TV, etc.).

   _____
   _____
   _____
   _____

3. List the top five concerns that you believe your spouse would identify in dealing with the children.

   _____
   _____
   _____
   _____

4. List the various ways you see or hear your spouse redirecting or parenting the children.

   _____
   _____
   _____
   _____

Exercise XX.A

5. For each concern you identified, describe what you want from your child(ren) (e.g., "Instead of fighting with his sister, I want him to cooperate or talk nicely to her").

   _____
   _____
   _____
   _____
   _____

6. At times it is easy to look back on how we may have handled a situation and say, "I should have . . ." Take time now to look back on how you would have changed the way you redirected or parented your children. Describe how you would have liked to intervene (e.g., "I should have realized when I was becoming increasingly aggravated. I could have taken a deep breath or told my spouse to take over because I needed a break").

   _____
   _____
   _____
   _____
   _____
   _____
   _____

7. As coparents, meet and exchange the responses to the prior six questions.

8. As coparents, record one list that describes your (meaning the two of you) list of expectations of each child in your home.

   *School expectations* (e.g., maintain a C average for all classes, do homework for 30 minutes a day): _____
   _____
   _____
   _____
   _____
   _____

   *Expectations regarding behavior with siblings and parents* (e.g., no cursing or smoking in the house): _____
   _____
   _____
   _____
   _____
   _____

Exercise XX.A

9. As coparents, brainstorm a list of possible *PRIVILEGES*\* for when expectations are met (e.g., "You will be able to stay on the phone until 9:00 P.M.").

   _____
   _____
   _____
   _____
   _____

10. Having an idea of what you want to have happen and what you will do if it happens is just part of the puzzle. The hard piece to fit in is following through in a relatively consistent manner. Take time now to reflect on times that you have tried this approach and have determined that it doesn't work. Describe what made you stop trying. In doing so, you will be identifying an area(s) in which you need support. This support will need to come from your partner or spouse (e.g., "The kids stopped trying," "They said they didn't care if they got to use the phone or not").

    _____
    _____
    _____
    _____
    _____

11. Describe how you will monitor when you are feeling like giving up and need support from your spouse/partner (e.g., "We will talk daily and rate our level of frustration tolerance").

    _____
    _____
    _____
    _____
    _____

12. Describe some ways you will provide support to your spouse or partner when he/she needs or requests it (e.g., "I will acknowledge my spouse's frustrations," "I will stay more actively involved in the parenting of *our* children").

    _____
    _____
    _____
    _____
    _____

---

\*Positive reinforcement inevitably works better than punishments and negative reinforcement.

Therapist's Overview

# WHAT'S THE MESSAGE I AM GIVING? WHAT'S THE MESSAGE I MEAN?

## GOALS OF THE EXERCISE

1. Parents identify ways in which they can negatively affect a child's self-worth by their comments.
2. Parents develop an understanding of when they are feeling frustrated or aggravated and say things that are derogatory.
3. Parents develop greater self-monitoring skills and an ability to focus their comments on a child's behavior and not his/her personhood.
4. Parents increase the amount of positive interactions between themselves and their children.

## ADDITIONAL HOMEWORK THAT MAY BE APPLICABLE TO PARENTING PROBLEMS

| | | |
|---|---|---|
| • Anger Control Problems | Go Blow Out Some Candles | Page 31 |
| • Caregiver Burnout | What Drawer Does This Belong In? | Page 74 |
| • Separation and Divorce | We Need to Agree | Page 231 |

## ADDITIONAL PROBLEMS IN WHICH THIS EXERCISE MAY BE USEFUL

- Single Parents

## SUGGESTIONS FOR PROCESSING THIS EXERCISE WITH THE CLIENT

Explain to parents in the group the power that parents' words have, especially negative words (e.g., "You're such a slob/lazy/stupid"). Talk about the various comments that parents can make that are negative and attack a child's self-worth. Generate a discussion of the negative feelings (e.g., frustration, anger, resentment, etc.) parents can experience when they are with their children and how it is common that during such times parents are more apt to be critical and attack a child's sense of self, regardless of it being unintentional. Describe that the purpose of the following exercise is to help them tune in to times that they may engage in such negative comments to their children and how they can make effective changes. You will probably need to stress that the purpose is *not* an attempt to make them feel guilty or to punish them in some way. Explain that this is not about blame but about identifying areas that can be changed to facilitate closer family relationships.

Exercise XX.B

# WHAT'S THE MESSAGE I AM GIVING?
# WHAT'S THE MESSAGE I MEAN?

As with any of us parents, we become frustrated at times with our children's behavior and we react and say things that we wish we could take back. For example, your daughter is acting very silly and doesn't know when to stop. You have had a long day at work and you just want her to stop, but she is not listening. You finally say, "Stop acting so stupid." Such comments may appear effective in stopping an unwanted behavior but can also create and reinforce a negative self-image within a child's mind. The purpose of the following exercise is to help you tune in to the triggers or situations and feelings you experience that make you more apt to respond in a negative way. You will also develop ways to more effectively and positively respond to your child or adolescent.

1. Over the next week, or in looking back over the past week, describe some of the situations in which you have made negative comments to your son or daughter. List these comments. It would be helpful for you to do this with your spouse or partner and generate a list together.

   _____
   _____
   _____
   _____
   _____
   _____

2. For each comment that you identified, describe the feelings and possible thoughts that your son or daughter might experience. A more effective way of completing this is by looking in the mirror or having your spouse or partner say the same comments to you.

   _____
   _____
   _____
   _____
   _____
   _____

Exercise XX.B

3. Ideally, the messages you are giving in these comments are not what you want to be saying to your son or daughter. For example, you don't want to be calling your daughter stupid for acting silly. You probably want her to know when enough is enough and to stop being silly. The primary difference is that the negative comment, "Stop being stupid," addresses your daughter's personhood instead of the behavior you want her to stop or change. For each negative comment you listed in item 1, write down what behavior you wanted to address.

_____
_____
_____
_____
_____
_____

4. Over the next week, try to keep aware of the behaviors that your children engage in and that concern you (e.g., "She is acting silly," "He is saying mean things to his sister or calling her names").

5. As coparents, make a list of the behaviors you identify over the course of the week.

_____
_____
_____
_____
_____
_____

6. In identifying the comments you listed in item 1, describe the situational factors and your feelings during such experiences.

_____
_____
_____
_____
_____
_____

7. The situations and feelings you just identified and described are the triggers to you making negative comments to your son or daughter. Over the next week keep track of whenever these situations and/or feelings arise.

_____
_____
_____
_____
_____

Exercise XX.B

8. The more aware you become of your triggers to making such negative comments, the more control you will develop over changing this.

9. As a way of replacing the negative comments, practice giving at least one positive or encouraging comment to each of your children every day over the next week. Record the times you do this in the following space and/or make a list of comments you could say over the next week.

_____
_____
_____
_____
_____
_____
_____
_____
_____
_____

Therapist's Overview

# COMPLIMENTS JAR

## GOALS OF THE EXERCISE

1. Increase the amount of positive interactions between parents and children.
2. Create a more positive environment within the family.
3. Increase the amount of validating each other's feelings.
4. Reinforce positive and/or desired behaviors.

## ADDITIONAL HOMEWORK THAT MAY BE APPLICABLE TO PARENTING PROBLEMS

- Anger Control Problems      Go Blow Out Some Candles           Page 31
- Caregiver Burnout           What Drawer Does This Belong In?   Page 74
- Separation and Divorce      We Need to Agree                   Page 231

## ADDITIONAL PROBLEMS IN WHICH THIS EXERCISE MAY BE USEFUL

- Single Parents

## SUGGESTIONS FOR PROCESSING THIS EXERCISE WITH THE CLIENT

This is a simple exercise to get families focused on the positive. Instruct group members to go home and label a jar of some kind as *The Compliments Jar*. Explain that they can use this jar to encourage and reinforce desired behaviors as well as create some fun and positive interactions among family members. The way to use the jar is to give someone a compliment or validate a person's feelings. Each time someone does this, they put their name, the comment they made, and to whom they directed it in the jar. At the end of each week or each day, the family gets together to count up the number of compliments put in the jar. As a reward, the person who put in the most gets to choose from a list of activities that they would like to do as a family. Explain that the greater number of compliments equals the bigger reward. The family will need to determine the various rewards and divide them up according to importance. The more important or valued rewards require a greater number of compliments. Also explain that each person has a quota to meet. Those who meet the quota have greater involvement in choosing the reward.

Exercise XX.C

# COMPLIMENTS JAR

This exercise is designed to encourage and reinforce desired behaviors, as well as create some fun and positive interactions among family members. The way to use the jar is to give someone a compliment, offer an encouraging statement, or validate a person's feelings. Each time someone does this, they put their name, the comment they made, and to whom they directed it in the jar. At the end of each week or each day, as a family you will need to come together to count up the number of compliments put in the jar. As a reward, the person who put in the most gets to choose from a list of activities that they would like to do as a family. Explain that the greater number of compliments equals the bigger reward. As a family, you will need to determine the various rewards and divide them up according to importance. The more important or valued rewards require a greater number of compliments. Each person will also be expected to meet a weekly or daily quota of compliments. Those who meet the quota will have a greater say in choosing the reward. The following steps will show you how to create and start using your Compliments Jar.

1. The first thing you will need to do is buy, or find in your home, a jar. It is preferable that the jar be clear so that you can see the number of compliments growing. The size should be approximately 1 gallon.

2. Label the jar as *The Compliments Jar,* or another name that you as a family choose.

3. Meet as a family and generate a list of family activities (e.g., playing a board game, going out for a walk, renting a video, going out to dinner, taking a vacation, etc.).

List of family activities

_____
_____
_____
_____
_____
_____
_____
_____
_____

Exercise XX.C

4. Break down the list of family activities into the following three categories:

| Fun reward | Better reward | Ultimate reward |
|---|---|---|
| Playing a board game as a family | Going out to eat as a family | Having a sleepover party |
| _____ | _____ | _____ |
| _____ | _____ | _____ |
| _____ | _____ | _____ |
| _____ | _____ | _____ |
| _____ | _____ | _____ |

5. Determine how many compliments, encouraging statements, or validating statements of another person's feelings are required for each category or type of reward. It is probably best to do this after one week of giving compliments, encouraging statements, and/or validating another person's feelings. After one week you will be able to get a baseline or expected number of compliments. For instance, if after one week, there are 50 compliments, encouraging statements, and/or validating statements, you could say that 30 in one week equals a *fun reward,* 50 will equal a *better reward,* and once you reach 100 (may take 1 or 2 weeks) the family can choose an *ultimate reward.*

Fun rewards require _____ compliments, encouraging statements, or validating statements.

Better rewards require _____ compliments, encouraging statements, or validating statements.

Ultimate rewards require _____ compliments, encouraging statements, or validating statements.

6. Brainstorm a list of possible compliments for each family member.

Family member: _____

_____
_____
_____
_____
_____
_____
_____
_____

Exercise XX.C

7. Have each person practice validating another person's feelings. Be sure to use an "I" statement in doing so. For example, "I can see (or get the sense) that you are very frustrated."
8. Start filling up your Compliments Jar!

*Another Version of The Compliments Jar*

You can also use this idea to address negative behavior. For example, every time your teenager curses, he/she must put a quarter in the jar. If you want to address smoking, you can charge 50 cents every time you detect or smell cigarette smoke.

Therapist's Overview

# WHAT ARE MY CHOICES?

## GOALS OF THE EXERCISE

1. Practice offering choices and establishing logical consequences.
2. Increase the amount of positive interactions between parents and children.
3. Create a more positive environment within the family.
4. Reinforce positive or desired behaviors.

## ADDITIONAL HOMEWORK THAT MAY BE APPLICABLE TO PARENTING PROBLEMS

| | | |
|---|---|---|
| • Anger Control Problems | Go Blow Out Some Candles | Page 31 |
| • Caregiver Burnout | What Drawer Does This Belong In? | Page 74 |
| • Separation and Divorce | We Need to Agree | Page 231 |

## ADDITIONAL PROBLEMS IN WHICH THIS EXERCISE MAY BE USEFUL

- Separation and Divorce
- Single Parents

## SUGGESTIONS FOR PROCESSING THIS EXERCISE WITH THE CLIENT

Explain to the group that parents frequently feel stuck in what they can do or say that will effectively redirect their children's undesired behavior. Describe that both parents need to be on the same page with what consequences are appropriate for which types of misbehavior and how these consequences should be implemented. Before assigning this homework, review the difference between natural consequences, which will result without parental involvement, and logical consequences, which are set by parents. Clarify or explain that logical consequences need to be related to the inappropriate behavior, implemented consistently, and presented without anger.

Exercise XX.D

# WHAT ARE MY CHOICES?

As parents we need to be aware of what choices we have in terms of ways to redirect our children's inappropriate behaviors. Children also need to be aware of what their choices are as a way of teaching them how to make proper decisions, as well as what is expected of them. The clearer we can be as parents, the fewer conflicts and misunderstandings we will have with our children. The purpose of the following exercise is to help you to learn to calmly set appropriate limits on a regular basis. Once you complete it, you should have a clearer picture of what you view as unacceptable behaviors by your children and, more important, what you view as appropriate (and that you want to see more of). You will be guided through a process of identifying consequences that fit the misbehavior and that can be enforced and presented without an angry tone.

1. As parents, make a list of behaviors that you consider inappropriate. For each inappropriate behavior, think about what makes it inappropriate and describe what the more acceptable or appropriate behavior would be. List the inappropriate and appropriate behaviors in the following spaces. For example:

   | **Inappropriate behavior** | **Appropriate behavior** |
   |---|---|
   | Coming home late | Coming home on time |

   **Inappropriate behavior**                **Appropriate behavior**

   _____                   _____
   _____                   _____
   _____                   _____
   _____                   _____
   _____                   _____
   _____                   _____
   _____                   _____

Exercise XX.D

2. Brainstorm a list of possible consequences. For example, "You will need to come home 30 minutes earlier tomorrow."

_____
_____
_____
_____
_____
_____
_____
_____
_____
_____

3. For each consequence you have listed, ask yourself the following questions:

| | | |
|---|---|---|
| Is this a logical consequence? | _____ Yes | _____ No |
| Is this age-appropriate? | _____ Yes | _____ No |
| Will I/we be able to follow through with it? | _____ Yes | _____ No |
| Can I present it calmly and without anger? | _____ Yes | _____ No |

4. Sometimes (a lot of times) our children can push us to the point of total frustration. As parents, we need to model for our children ways to manage our anger and frustration. One way to do this is by rating our level. For example, your son does not heed your request to pick up his coat. On a scale of 1 to 10 (10 equals the boiling point), you feel about a 3. You ask him again, and he ignores your request again or says, "In a minute." You can feel yourself becoming angry. Your heart may start pounding harder, your voice may start to deepen or raise in volume, and so forth. At this point your level may be at a 6. By becoming aware of our anger and frustration level, we can interrupt a situation that is bound to explode (chances are that as you become more frustrated and louder, your son will react in a similar way, resulting in a shouting match). As a couple, identify situations that are likely to put your level rating at 6 or higher. List such situations in the following spaces.

_____
_____
_____
_____
_____
_____
_____

Exercise XX.D

5. Knowing ahead of time which situations tend to push your buttons the most gives you an advantage over interrupting the escalating cycle of conflict between you and your children. As a couple discuss the preceding situations and ways that you can redirect your own anger and frustration. How might you work as a team in such situations (when possible)? List your ideas in the following spaces.

_____
_____
_____
_____
_____
_____
_____
_____

6. Share your ideas of redirecting anger and frustration with your group. By sharing, you will each learn of additional ideas for you to try.

# Section XXI

# PHOBIAS—SPECIFIC/SOCIAL

Therapist's Overview

# I CAN PICTURE IT

## GOALS OF THE EXERCISE

1. Develop a way of decreasing stress and anxiety.
2. Learn the basics of deep breathing.
3. Learn the basics of visualization.

## ADDITIONAL HOMEWORK THAT MAY BE APPLICABLE TO PHOBIAS—SPECIFIC/SOCIAL

| | | |
|---|---|---|
| • Agoraphobia/Panic | Breaking My Panic Cycle | Page 14 |
| • Anxiety | What Happens When I Feel Anxious? | Page 36 |
| • Anxiety | Beating Self-Defeating Beliefs | Page 42 |
| • Depression | Taking Charge of Your Thoughts | Page 126 |

## ADDITIONAL PROBLEMS IN WHICH THIS EXERCISE MAY BE USEFUL

- Anxiety
- Anger Control Problems
- Depression

## SUGGESTIONS FOR PROCESSING THIS EXERCISE WITH THE CLIENT

This exercise will help group members practice deep breathing and visualization as a way of decreasing their stress and anxiety. Practice both techniques with them first in group before assigning this task.

Exercise XXI.A

# I CAN PICTURE IT

This exercise will help you to practice the deep breathing exercises and visualizations you learned in group.

1. Sit in a comfortable (not too comfortable) chair and close your eyes.
2. Put one hand on your stomach and one hand on your chest
3. Take a slow deep breath in through your nose.
4. Picture a balloon in your stomach that you will be inflating with each inhalation. If the hand on your chest is moving and the hand on your stomach is not, you are not breathing in deep enough.
5. Exhale slowly through your mouth. Pretend that you are blowing out a candle. You could picture 10 individual candles in front of you. With each exhale blow out one candle.
6. With each exhale you may want to repeat a calming statement to yourself (e.g., "I am calm," "I am okay," "I am relaxed," etc.).
7. Once you have blown out all 10 candles, picture a place where you feel totally safe.
8. Describe that safe place in as much detail as possible in the following space. You could describe the temperature, what you see when you look around, any smells or sounds, and so forth.

   _____
   _____
   _____
   _____
   _____
   _____
   _____

9. Imagine that you are at your safe place. Describe how good it feels to be there.

   _____
   _____
   _____
   _____

10. Practice the deep breathing and visualization of your safe place at least once a day.

Therapist's Overview

# HOW DOES THIS HAPPEN?

## GOALS OF THE EXERCISE

1. Develop a clear understanding of the triggering events that lead to fear and panic.
2. Develop a clear understanding of current triggers to fear and panic.
3. Focus in on the phobic anxiety attack cycle.

## ADDITIONAL HOMEWORK THAT MAY BE APPLICABLE TO PHOBIAS—SPECIFIC/SOCIAL

| | | |
|---|---|---|
| • Agoraphobia/Panic | When Is This Going to Happen? | Page 12 |
| • Anxiety | What Else Can I Say or Do? | Page 39 |

## ADDITIONAL PROBLEMS IN WHICH THIS EXERCISE MAY BE USEFUL

- Anger Control Problems
- Anxiety
- Depression
- Phobias—Specific/Social

## SUGGESTIONS FOR PROCESSING THIS EXERCISE WITH THE CLIENT

Individuals suffering with fear and panic often describe how such overwhelming emotions suddenly appear without warning. Explain to the group that many times they can learn to recognize the warning signs. In doing so, they will acquire greater control over their fears. This exercise will work best if you discuss in session some of the members' first experiences and phobic responses. Guide them through the process of identifying some possible thoughts and physical sensations that they have experienced. Also, help them to focus in on their surroundings when they were experiencing the fear and anxiety. Where were they? What was the weather like? What did the room look like?

**Exercise XXI.B**

# HOW DOES THIS HAPPEN?

This exercise will help you to key into the events that contribute to you feeling fear, anxiety, and panic. You will need to think about the first time your felt panic as well as some recent time. In becoming more familiar with your response (physical, emotional, cognitive), you will develop greater control over your panic and be able to take back your life.

1. Describe the first time that you felt panic.

   Where were you?
   _____

   Who was with you?
   _____

   What time of day was it?
   _____

   What were you doing or planning to do?
   _____
   _____
   _____

   How long ago did this first time take place?
   _____

   How often have you been experiencing fear and/or panic in the last month?
   _____

   How similar are the situational factors to you experiencing anxiety and fear of panic now as compared with the first time? If they are different, describe in what way they are different.
   _____
   _____
   _____
   _____
   _____

Exercise XXI.B

2. Write a statement describing how much you want to defeat and overcome these fears and panic. For example, "This is the worst thing in the world and I have to get rid of these feelings. I am ready to do whatever it takes."

   _____
   _____

3. Think about the last time that you felt like you were going to have a panic attack (or did have an attack), describe the physical sensations you experienced (e.g., sweaty palms, weak or shaky knees, lightheadedness, heart pounding, shortness of breath, etc.).

   _____
   _____
   _____

4. What did you think would happen at that time?

   _____
   _____

   What were you thinking about after this happened and you had calmed down?

   _____
   _____
   _____

5. What is the worst thing that could happen to you during one of these episodes?

   _____
   _____

6. In answering the preceding questions, you have defined your anxiety attack cycle. This involves the triggers to feeling anxious (item 1), the physical signs (item 3), and the negative thoughts that tend to intensify the situation (items 4 and 5).

7. Over the next week keep track of times that this cycle becomes activated. It is generally better for you to record the situation and the phases of the cycle on paper or in a notebook. Bring this to your next group session.

Therapist's Overview

# LET'S FLOAT WITH IT

## GOALS OF THE EXERCISE

1. Develop a personal anxiety thermometer or scale in order to gauge and recognize when the feeling of anxiety is increasing.
2. Practice acknowledging, observing, and being able to float with the feelings of panic when they occur.
3. Develop a list of self-soothing and more adaptive coping statements.

## ADDITIONAL HOMEWORK THAT MAY BE APPLICABLE TO PHOBIAS—SPECIFIC/SOCIAL

- Agoraphobia/Panic — Breaking My Panic Cycle — Page 14
- Anxiety — What Happens When I Feel Anxious? — Page 36
- Anxiety — Beating Self-Defeating Beliefs — Page 42
- Depression — Taking Charge of Your Thoughts — Page 126

## ADDITIONAL PROBLEMS IN WHICH THIS EXERCISE MAY BE USEFUL

- Anger Control Problems
- Anxiety
- Phobia—Specific/Social

## SUGGESTIONS FOR PROCESSING THIS EXERCISE WITH THE CLIENT

One way to introduce this exercise is to describe to the group the need to increase self-monitoring skills as a way to overcome anxiety. Have them practice rating different situations that they have experienced in the past week. Utilize visualization as an intervention and have the group visualize a thermometer or rating scale (1 to 10), which they can use to gauge their level of anxiety. Another visualization to review is having the group members imagine floating with the feeling. Describe how panic is like a wave and that it comes over you sometimes very strong like a tidal wave, but always leaves. Remind them that the wave never lasts forever. It comes and goes. It will also be important for you to review common thinking errors and alternative coping statements. (See the exercise, "Taking Charge of Your Thoughts," in Section XII, "Depression.") Have group members record the various types of thinking errors or cognitive distortions. It would be best if you could give them a list with definitions and a space for them to record an example of each one.

Exercise XXI.C

# LET'S FLOAT WITH IT

The purpose of this exercise is threefold. One purpose is to help you identify the level of anxiety or fear that you are experiencing when you are experiencing it. Rating such experiences will allow you to differentiate experiences and help you to avoid lumping all situations as panic attacks. Developing a habit of rating such situations will also help you to recognize when your anxiety is present and provide a window of opportunity for you to intervene. The second purpose is for you to increase your comfort level of "floating" with the feelings of anxiety. By floating, I mean realizing that anxiety is like any other feeling and that it comes and goes. The more you realize that such feelings *do end and leave,* the more success you will have in overcoming such fears and related feelings. The third purpose is for you to identify some of the contributing negative thoughts in which you engage when you feel anxious. By identifying these negative thoughts, you have the ability to rewrite such beliefs. Learning what you can say instead of, "This is it, I am going to die," will help you manage times you feel uncomfortable.

1. Over the next few days, take a break from your daily life and rate your level of anxiety. You can do this on the hour or periodically throughout the day (e.g., when you wake up, at lunch, at dinner, and before you go to bed). You can rate your anxiety on a scale of 1 to 10. Let 1 represent little if any anxiety and 10 represent having a panic attack. You can use a diary, notebook, appointment book, or something similar.

2. Once you have taken recordings and ratings for a few days, review the times that you gave a rating of 6 or higher. Describe those situation(s) by answering the following questions:

Where were you?
_____

Who was with you?
_____

What time of day was it?
_____

What were you doing or planning to do?
_____

Describe the physical sensations you experienced (e.g., sweaty palms, weak or shaky knees, lightheadedness, heart pounding, shortness of breath, etc.).

What were some of the thoughts you had during this time?

3. Review your list of thinking errors and identify which ones you were engaging in.

4. For each thinking error you just listed, write one or two alternative and more adaptive statements that you could say to yourself.

5. Review your list of recordings and ratings. For those situations that you rated between 3 and 6, try to relive them by thinking about each one in a step-by-step fashion. Think about where you were when you started to feel anxious, think and try to feel the physical sensations you experienced. Last, try to repeat some of the negative thoughts you had. As you are doing this, repeat the alternative thoughts and statements you just wrote (item 4). In recalling each of these situations, imagine yourself floating with the feeling. Remind yourself that the feeling will pass, and that it always has.

6. Each day, practice floating with those situations that you would rate at a low to moderate level (e.g., under 6). Record your experiences and discuss in your next group session.

**Therapist's Overview**

# I CAN DO THIS

## GOALS OF THE EXERCISE

1. Decrease your level of anxiety.
2. Build confidence in your own ability to handle anxiety-producing situations.
3. Complete in vivo experiences successfully.

## ADDITIONAL HOMEWORK THAT MAY BE APPLICABLE TO PHOBIAS—SPECIFIC/SOCIAL

- Agoraphobia/Panic Breaking My Panic Cycle Page 14
- Anxiety What Happens When I Feel Anxious? Page 36
- Anxiety Beating Self-Defeating Beliefs Page 42
- Depression Taking Charge of Your Thoughts Page 126

## ADDITIONAL PROBLEMS IN WHICH THIS EXERCISE MAY BE USEFUL

- Anxiety
- Assertiveness Deficit

## SUGGESTIONS FOR PROCESSING THIS EXERCISE WITH THE CLIENT

This exercise should be introduced after group members have been exposed to visualization, deep breathing, and ways to redirect thinking errors. The purpose of the exercise is to give group members experience in putting such interventions to work outside of your office or their homes.

**Exercise XXI.D**

# I CAN DO THIS

In completing this exercise, you will be able to prove to yourself that you can overcome your fears. You will be using the visualization or guided imagery and deep breathing and relaxation techniques you have learned thus far in therapy. In addition, you will need to put into practice challenging your thinking errors and redirecting such negative thoughts. *You can do this.*

1. Generate a hierarchy list from least to most anxiety provoking.

   _____
   _____
   _____
   _____
   _____
   _____
   _____
   _____
   _____
   _____
   _____

2. Pick the least anxiety-provoking experience you have listed, and write a goal for being able to overcome it. For example, "I will walk around the block once before dinner today."

   _____
   _____

3. Identify at least three coping statements that you will use.

   _____
   _____
   _____
   _____

4. Remember to practice deep breathing exercises before and during.
5. You can first try this with the assistance of a support person, if you need it, but after one or two times, you should do it on your own.
6. Rate your level of anxiety before and after.

7. Increase the amount of time and/or frequency you tried this desensitization exercise. For example, if you walked to the corner two times, tomorrow do it four times. If you went to a pet shop and looked at the snakes for two minutes, go tomorrow and watch them for four or five minutes.
8. Each time that you attempt the desensitization exercise, be sure to reward yourself for your courage.
9. Once you have achieved your goal and your anxiety level rating is under 2, pick the next anxiety-provoking situation you have listed on your hierarchy. Repeat steps 2 through 8.

# Section XXII

# RAPE SURVIVORS

**Therapist's Overview**

# SHARING MY STORY

## GOALS OF THE EXERCISE

1. Begin a process of healing.
2. Realize that by getting it out, one can start to let it go.
3. Begin to realize, by sharing your story with the group and listening to the others' stories, that you are not alone.
4. Begin to acknowledge the feelings of pain, anger, hurt, and so on that are associated with the sexual assault.

## ADDITIONAL HOMEWORK THAT MAY BE APPLICABLE TO RAPE SURVIVORS

- Anger Control Problems     My Safe Place              Page 33
- Depression                 My Feelings Journal        Page 123
- Incest Survivors—Adult     My Story                   Page 175
- Incest Survivors—Adult     What I Need to Tell You    Page 179
- Phobias—Specific/Social    I Can Picture It           Page 207

## ADDITIONAL PROBLEMS IN WHICH THIS EXERCISE MAY BE USEFUL

- Domestic Violence Survivors
- Incest Survivors—Adult
- Toxic Parent Survivors

## SUGGESTIONS FOR PROCESSING THIS EXERCISE WITH THE CLIENT

Explain to the group that each person has a story to tell and that, more important, each member of the group deserves to be heard. This sharing can begin the process of healing. Let members know that by putting down on paper and then being able to verbalize what happened to them, the process of letting go of and overcoming what happened begins.

Exercise XXII.A

# SHARING MY STORY

Although you may never forget what happened to you, *you can* put it behind you. One of the ways of healing involves being able to tell what happened. In doing so, you begin to take back control. Being able to write about and share what happened releases you from the feeling of being trapped and controlled. This exercise will walk you through and get you started on the road to healing by helping you give voice to what happened.

1. How old were you when you were assaulted?

   _____

2. Was the person who assaulted you a stranger, an acquaintance, a relative, or a friend?

   _____

3. How old was this person?

   _____

4. Where were you when the assault took place?

   _____

5. Who else, if anyone, was around? Where were they?

   _____

6. How long did the assault last?

   _____

7. What did the person say to you, if anything, while he/she assaulted you?

   _____
   _____

8. How did you know when it was over? What happened?

   _____
   _____

9. Describe what the person said or did when it was over.

   _____
   _____

Exercise XXII.A

10. What were you thinking and feeling while the assault was taking place?

11. What were you thinking and feeling after the assault?

12. What was the worst aspect of the assault?

13. How has the assault affected you in your daily life (eating, sleeping, concentration, work, relationships with family, friends, romantic partners)?

14. How has the assault affected your view of yourself?

15. What is the hardest part regarding the assault for you to overcome?

16. What are some of your positive qualities and characteristics that will help you to become a survivor instead of a victim?

Therapist's Overview

# CHANGING MY FAULTY THINKING

## GOALS OF THE EXERCISE

1. Identify some of the distorted and faulty thinking.
2. Identify at least two alternative thoughts or self-statements for each negative thought.
3. Improve outlook on life in general and on self.

## ADDITIONAL HOMEWORK THAT MAY BE APPLICABLE TO RAPE SURVIVORS

- Anger Control Problems — My Safe Place — Page 33
- Depression — My Feelings Journal — Page 123
- Incest Survivors—Adult — My Story — Page 175
- Incest Survivors—Adult — What I Need to Tell You — Page 179
- Phobias—Specific/Social — I Can Picture It — Page 207

## ADDITIONAL PROBLEMS IN WHICH THIS EXERCISE MAY BE USEFUL

- Domestic Violence Survivors
- Incest Survivors—Adult
- Toxic Parent Survivors

## SUGGESTIONS FOR PROCESSING THIS EXERCISE WITH THE CLIENT

This exercise is geared toward individuals identifying and restructuring negative thoughts or thinking errors. It is best to review some of the negative thoughts in which group members engage to normalize the problem. Group members will need to know that others engage in such thinking. Explain to the group the power of their thoughts and the benefits of cognitive restructuring. In having a list of alternative thoughts, group members will never be without options in terms of redirecting their thoughts in a positive direction.

Exercise XXII.B

# CHANGING MY FAULTY THINKING

Our thoughts are extremely powerful. When we engage in negative thinking, it frequently leads to negative feelings. This exercise is designed to help you change the negative thoughts you might repeat to yourself and identify alternative and more self-adaptive thoughts and statements. The following list is based on the thoughts and beliefs held and reported frequently by others who have also been assaulted. Add any other negative thoughts that are not on the list. Most important, see if you can offer alternative and more positive thoughts and beliefs for each faulty or negative one listed. For each negative statement, identify two positive and more self-adaptive statements.

| Negative or faulty beliefs or thoughts | More self-adaptive statements and thoughts |
|---|---|
| 1. It was my fault. | |
| 2. I can't trust others. | |
| 3. I can't trust myself. | |
| 4. I am bad. | |
| 5. My body betrayed me. | |
| 6. I can't protect myself. | |
| 7. Sex is dirty. | |
| 8. I have to be in control. | |

**Others that you can think of:**

9. _____

10. _____

11. _____

12. _____

13. _____

14. _____

15. _____

16. _____

Therapist's Overview

# WHAT I FEEL AND WHAT I THINK

## GOALS OF THE EXERCISE

1. Express your thoughts and feelings regarding the assault and the person who assaulted you.
2. Begin to develop a sense of empowerment over the assault.

## ADDITIONAL HOMEWORK THAT MAY BE APPLICABLE TO RAPE SURVIVORS

| | | |
|---|---|---|
| • Anger Control Problems | My Safe Place | Page 33 |
| • Depression | My Feelings Journal | Page 123 |
| • Incest Survivors—Adult | My Story | Page 175 |
| • Incest Survivors—Adult | What I Need to Tell You | Page 179 |
| • Phobias—Specific/Social | I Can Picture It | Page 207 |

## ADDITIONAL PROBLEMS IN WHICH THIS EXERCISE MAY BE USEFUL

- Domestic Violence Survivors
- Incest Survivors—Adult
- Toxic Parent Survivors

## SUGGESTIONS FOR PROCESSING THIS EXERCISE WITH THE CLIENT

Once group members have been able to discuss the assault and process some of their thoughts and feelings, individuals may feel a sense of empowerment by writing a letter to their attacker. This letter does not need to be sent. Once group members have written their letter, you may want to empower them further by having them engage in an empty-chair technique. In using an empty chair, they can imagine reading the letter aloud to the person who attacked them. This may be difficult for some. One way to make them feel more comfortable is by having them imagine that slabs of Plexiglas exist between the empty chair and themselves.

**Exercise XXII.C**

# WHAT I FEEL AND WHAT I THINK

Once you have been able to identify and discuss some of your thoughts and feelings about the assault, you may feel ready to write a letter to your attacker. This letter is not intended for you to send. The purpose is more for you to be able to express your thoughts and feelings to that person indirectly and safely. Once you have written it, you can share your letter in the next group session.

In writing the letter, keep the following in mind:

- How the assault made you feel about yourself and your body.
- Concerns you had regarding what others would think.
- How the assault has affected your relationships with others.
- How it has affected your perception of the world, men, and people.
- How it affected your daily life initially and presently.

Most important, keep in mind and describe the following:

- How you have become a survivor.
- Why the effects of the abuse no longer control you or have power over you like they once did.
- How you feel about the person who assaulted you.
- What you think of that person.
- What you think should happen to that person.

If you have been able to identify, verbalize, and discuss your feelings of anger, pain, resentment, frustration, and other similar feelings, you may want to consider the process of forgiveness. Before considering this, it is important to realize and accept that the responsibility for the assault lies *completely* with the person who assaulted you. If you have been able to forgive that person, you might include a few comments regarding this. Sometimes through forgiveness, you will find peace and closure.

# Section XXIII

# SEPARATION AND DIVORCE

**Therapist's Overview**

# TALKING TO THE CHILDREN

## GOALS OF THE EXERCISE

1. Make a commitment to upholding the best interest of the children through the divorce process.
2. Identify what and how to tell the children about the divorce.

## ADDITIONAL HOMEWORK THAT MAY BE APPLICABLE TO SEPARATION AND DIVORCE

- Parenting Problems        Working from the Same Page        Page 190
- Single Parents        Single Parenting—Pro or Con?        Page 248

## ADDITIONAL PROBLEMS IN WHICH THIS EXERCISE MAY BE USEFUL

- Grief/Loss Unresolved

## SUGGESTIONS FOR PROCESSING THIS EXERCISE WITH THE CLIENT

Individuals contemplating what to tell their children regarding getting a divorce need to have a plan in order to minimize the fallout of such news. In group it will be important to review the various developmental stages of children so that group members will be better equipped in preparing to talk with their children. It will also be beneficial for you to have the group practice different approaches to talking with their children. Once they have practiced this and have heard others do the same, they will have a clearer idea of what they actually will say and how. The following exercise is designed to help individuals formulate a plan for doing this in vivo. It will also be helpful for individuals to share with their soon-to-be former spouse, so as to provide an opportunity for both parents to be on the same page.

Exercise XXIII.A

# TALKING TO THE CHILDREN

This exercise is designed to help you put in writing what and how you want to tell your children about the divorce. If your spouse is not attending the same group, you can share this exercise to help you both to be on the same page in talking with your children. Utilize the group experience of practicing what you might want to say and how. Once you have done so, complete the following exercise.

1. Where will you be when you tell them the news?
   _____

2. Who will be with you?
   _____

3. Will you tell the children individually or as a group?
   _____

4. How will you answer the following questions if your children ask?

   Why are you getting a divorce?
   _____
   _____
   _____
   _____

   When will it happen?
   _____

   Where will I be living?
   _____

   When will I see my brother(s), sister(s), other parent, friends, and so forth?
   _____
   _____
   _____

   Did I do something wrong?
   _____

Exercise XXIII.A

Don't you love each other anymore?
_____

Do you love me anymore?
_____

List other questions that you think they may ask.
_____
_____
_____
_____
_____
_____
_____
_____

Therapist's Overview

# WE NEED TO AGREE*

## GOALS OF THE EXERCISE

1. Parents agree to cooperate and work together in the best interest of the children.
2. Children feel greater security and a sense of stability.

## ADDITIONAL HOMEWORK THAT MAY BE APPLICABLE TO SEPARATION AND DIVORCE

- Parenting Problems         Working from the Same Page        Page 190
- Single Parents             Single Parenting—Pro or Con?      Page 248

## ADDITIONAL PROBLEMS IN WHICH THIS EXERCISE MAY BE USEFUL

- Blended Families[†]

## SUGGESTIONS FOR PROCESSING THIS EXERCISE WITH THE CLIENT

A common difficulty among divorcing parents is acting as a unified team. Explain the importance of working together in order to minimize the negative effects on the children. Although this is no easy task, it is recommended that you suggest that parents create a contract that both sign in order to reinforce their commitment of getting along for the sake of the children. The following exercise will help them to create an example of a contract, which addresses the areas of visitation, house rules at both parents' houses, expectations regarding school work, and expectations of behavior of each family member.

---

*This exercise was first described by Bevilacqua, L., & Dattilio, F. (2001) *Brief Family Therapy Homework Planner.* New York: John Wiley & Sons.

[†]Note: This is not a problem identified in this Homework Planner.

Exercise XXIII.B

# WE NEED TO AGREE

Divorcing is never easy and carries numerous conflicts and struggles. You can reduce some of these difficulties by deciding on how you can work together for the sake of the children. As parents, it is especially important for you both to be on the same page with each other. Whether you are married to each other or not, you are both still parents to your children. One of the ways you can make things easier on yourself as well as the rest of the family is to work together. You are probably saying, "If we could do that we wouldn't have gotten divorced!" You are right, but sometimes it can actually be easier to work together when you are no longer married or living with each other. The following exercise is designed to help you start the process of working together to reduce your own level of stress (as well as everyone else's).

1. Complete the following schedule for visitation.

|  | Sunday | Monday | Tuesday | Wednesday | Thursday | Friday | Saturday |
|---|---|---|---|---|---|---|---|
| Pick-up time |  |  |  |  |  |  |  |
| Drop-off time |  |  |  |  |  |  |  |

Once you have agreed on this schedule, give a copy to each child and keep one for yourself.

2. Identify house rules (i.e., "Dinner is at 6:00 P.M.," "Curfew is 9:00 P.M.," "Homework is to be done before you go outside or have friends over"). The more that your house rules match up with your former spouse's, the more consistency there is (and less confusion) for your children. A copy of the house rules should then be given to each child, keeping one for yourself.

**Dad's house rules**

A. _____
B. _____
C. _____
D. _____

Exercise XXIII.B

E. _____
F. _____
G. _____

**Mom's house rules**

A. _____
B. _____
C. _____
D. _____
E. _____
F. _____
G. _____

Ideally, these two lists can be traded in for one list: "Parents' house rules."

3. Describe your expectations for school (i.e., "You need to maintain at least a C average in all of your subjects"; "Homework is to be done before any social activities"). Your children should also be able to voice their input to this. *Each child should have his/her own list of expectations.*

**Dad's expectations for school**

A. _____
B. _____
C. _____
D. _____
E. _____

**Mom's expectations for school**

A. _____
B. _____
C. _____
D. _____
E. _____

Ideally, these two lists can be traded in for one list: "Parents' expectations for school."

Exercise XXIII.B

4. Describe the type of behavior you expect of each other (this includes parents with kids as well as kids with parents) (e.g., "When we speak to each other, we are to speak calmly and with an inside voice and without any cursing or name-calling").

**Dad's expectations of how we should treat each other**

A. _____
B. _____
C. _____
D. _____
E. _____
F. _____
G. _____

**Mom's expectations of how we should treat each other**

A. _____
B. _____
C. _____
D. _____
E. _____
F. _____
G. _____

Ideally, these two lists can be traded in for one list: "Parents' expectations of how we should treat each other."

Therapist's Overview

# SAYING GOOD-BYE AND SAYING HELLO

## GOALS OF THE EXERCISE

1. Identify and express the various thoughts and feelings you have regarding the divorce.
2. Develop a sense of strength and be able to let go of your former partner.
3. Identify sources of support (people as well as activities).

## ADDITIONAL HOMEWORK THAT MAY BE APPLICABLE TO SEPARATION AND DIVORCE

- Parenting Problems         Working from the Same Page         Page 190
- Single Parents             Single Parenting—Pro or Con?       Page 248

## ADDITIONAL PROBLEMS IN WHICH THIS EXERCISE MAY BE USEFUL

- Single Parents

## SUGGESTIONS FOR PROCESSING THIS EXERCISE WITH THE CLIENT

This exercise is designed to give individuals a chance to put in writing their thoughts and feelings regarding the marriage, the divorce, and how they have managed to move on. This is particularly helpful for individuals who have progressed somewhat through the process of grief regarding the marriage. Completing this will in some way serve as closure by being able to say good-bye to their former spouse and say hello to their new life as a single parent.

Exercise XXIII.C

# SAYING GOOD-BYE AND SAYING HELLO

This exercise is designed to facilitate your being able to say good-bye to your former spouse and say hello to your new life as a single parent or remarried parent. In doing this, you will hopefully feel a sense of closure. What you will be doing is writing a letter describing your thoughts and feelings regarding the relationship and the divorce. You will also be identifying the various support systems and strategies you are using or will be using to maintain your ability to move on.

1. Take some time to think about and write down how you first met and eventually got married.

2. What was or is good about your former spouse and the relationship you shared?

3. When did the relationship become so conflictual that you began to consider divorce?

Exercise XXIII.C

4. With which aspects of how you and your former spouse proceeded with the divorce process do you feel the most anger and resentment?

5. What about it makes you feel sad?

6. In what do you find the most relief when you think about no longer being married to your former spouse?

7. What fears and worries do you have regarding being divorced?

8. What other feelings or thoughts do you have regarding getting or being divorced?

9. How will being divorced be better for you?

Exercise XXIII.C

10. What are you doing differently, or planning to do differently, that will make your life better now or once you are no longer living with your former spouse (e.g., social activities, hobbies, etc.)?

    _____
    _____
    _____
    _____

11. What individuals make up your support network?

    _____
    _____
    _____
    _____

12. How often are you connecting with your support network (e.g., by phone, e-mail, in person, etc.)?

    _____

13. When is the next time that you will be touching base with one of the people in your support network?

    _____

# Section XXIV

# SHYNESS

Therapist's Overview

# THREE KEY INGREDIENTS TO POSITIVE SOCIAL INTERACTIONS

## GOALS OF THE EXERCISE

1. Increase the amount of social interaction skills.
2. Increase the amount of comfort in social settings.
3. Increase the positive thoughts of oneself and ability to be in social situations.

## ADDITIONAL HOMEWORK THAT MAY BE APPLICABLE TO SHYNESS

- Anxiety                      Beating Self-Defeating Beliefs     Page 42
- Assertiveness Deficit        It's Okay to Be Assertive          Page 51

## ADDITIONAL PROBLEMS IN WHICH THIS EXERCISE MAY BE USEFUL

- Anxiety

## SUGGESTIONS FOR PROCESSING THIS EXERCISE WITH THE CLIENT

Overcoming shyness requires increasing the amount of exposure in social situations. Develop a hierarchy of such situations with each group member. Review the process of deep breathing and positive thinking or cognitive restructuring of negative thoughts. Once group members have a basic understanding and some practice within the group setting of breathing deeply and redirecting negative thoughts, let them know that they will need to try some in vivo exercises. The purpose of the following exercise is to have group members practice key social skills that will help them feel more comfortable and confident in social settings, while utilizing the deep breathing and cognitive techniques.

Exercise XXIV.A

# THREE KEY INGREDIENTS TO POSITIVE SOCIAL INTERACTIONS

Knowing what to say or do in social situations takes work and skills, which each of us need to know about. The following exercise is designed to help you practice some of the key ingredients to positive interactions with others over the next seven days.

1. Most people prefer to be around others who are happy or in a good mood. One of the easiest ways to project this is with a *smile*. Therefore, one key skill to practice over the next three days is to smile at three different people each day. That means you will smile at least nine times over the next three days *and* someone else will see you doing it.

2. For someone to see you smile and for you to know that they saw you, you need to make some kind of *eye contact*. Therefore, another key skill to practice over the next three days is to look at these three different people each day for the next three days.

3. Once you have practiced these two key skills, write about your experience (e.g., Who did you look at and smile? What was their reaction?).

   _____
   _____
   _____
   _____

4. For days four, five, and six, if you have not already done so, try to *say hi* to someone. You will need to look at that person and smile first, and then just say "Hi." Most people will just say "Hi" right back, or they may say, "How are you?" You do not need to engage in any lengthy conversation. Just say "Hi" as you walk by someone. Try to do this two to three times each day for the next three days.

5. After each day that you have said "Hi," write about your experience.

   _____
   _____
   _____
   _____

6. On the seventh day, relax. Read over your experiences from the week. Congratulate yourself on your efforts.

Therapist's Overview

# WHAT COMES AFTER "HI"?

## GOALS OF THE EXERCISE

1. Add to your list of social interaction skills.
2. Increase your comfort level in social situations.
3. Increase your awareness of the many topics available for conversation starters.

## ADDITIONAL HOMEWORK THAT MAY BE APPLICABLE TO SHYNESS

- Anxiety      Beating Self-Defeating Beliefs      Page 42
- Assertiveness Deficit      It's Okay to Be Assertive      Page 51

## ADDITIONAL PROBLEMS IN WHICH THIS EXERCISE MAY BE USEFUL

- Anxiety

## SUGGESTIONS FOR PROCESSING THIS EXERCISE WITH THE CLIENT

A frequent concern voiced by individuals who are shy is that they don't know what to talk about to others. A primary yet underlying factor involved in this anxiety is their fear of embarrassing themselves or feeling like others are judging them negatively. The following exercise is designed to address both of these issues. The goal is to help individuals develop a grab bag of ideas and topics to talk with others about, as well as decrease or restructure the negative self-talk that goes on in their heads.

Exercise XXIV.B

# WHAT COMES AFTER "HI"?

Not knowing what to say when you are with others can create a tremendous amount of discomfort and anxiety. An additional factor that maintains this anxiety involves various types of negative self-talk that most of us engage in from time to time. When we are not sure of what to say to others and we are telling ourselves, "Better be quiet or I'll just end up making a fool out of myself," the chance of feeling anxious and not talking with others is rather high. The following exercise has been designed as a way for you to address this problem. There are two goals intended in completing the following exercise: (1) to generate a list of various topics or subjects that you feel comfortable with, and (2) to redirect the negative self-talk.

1. To increase your knowledge of current events and to have a handful of topics available for you to discuss in social situations, follow the following instructions for the next two days.

    - Read at least three articles in your local newspaper.
    - Watch 30 minutes of a news broadcast
    - Read at least three articles in a magazine.

    You may want to summarize each of the topics you have read about or heard about.

    _____
    _____
    _____
    _____
    _____
    _____
    _____
    _____
    _____
    _____
    _____
    _____
    _____
    _____
    _____

2. Make a list of the different topics or subjects you like or interests that you have.

   _____
   _____
   _____
   _____
   _____
   _____
   _____

   This list and those articles you read about or heard about are just the beginning of filling your grab bag of conversation starters and joiners. Continue reading magazines and the newspaper or any other material on topics that interest you. Watching the news or watching television programs that your coworkers and/or friends may like will also provide you with more information to join in on or start conversations.

3. The second part of this exercise is to address the negative self-talk. You may be saying things like:

   - My coworkers or friends don't have the same interests that I do.
   - I can never remember things I read about or saw on the news.
   - Whatever I say never comes out right. It's better for me to just be quiet.

4. What other comments have crossed your mind?

   _____
   _____
   _____

5. Challenging and replacing or restructuring our thoughts takes lots of practice. To start with, for each comment that goes through your mind that is negative or self-defeating, record an alternative comment. For example:

   *Negative self-defeating comment.* "My coworkers or friends don't have the same interests that I do."

   *Alternative comment.* "Although my friends and coworkers don't like everything I like, we do have some common interests."

   *Negative self-defeating comment.* "I can never remember things I read about or saw on the news."

   *Alternative comment.* "It is hard to remember everything I read about or saw on the news. Maybe I could write down some key points to help me remember."

Exercise XXIV.B

Use the following lines to record your negative self-defeating and alternative comments.

*Negative self-defeating comment.* _____

*Alternative comment.* _____

*Negative self-defeating comment.* _____

*Alternative comment.* _____

*Negative self-defeating comment.* _____

*Alternative comment.* _____

*Negative self-defeating comment.* _____

*Alternative comment.* _____

*Negative self-defeating comment.* _____

*Alternative comment.* _____

*Negative self-defeating comment.* _____

*Alternative comment.* _____

6. Writing these alternative comments is just the start. You must also practice saying them so that they become the type of thought that runs through your mind instead of the negative self-defeating comments. Practice repeating the alternative comments at least three times a day over the next several days.

Exercise XXIV.B

7. As you think of or hear of other alternative comments, add them to your list and practice them as well. The more you practice these alternative comments the more natural they will become and the more positive you will be.

8. Another way to feel more positive about yourself is by practicing daily affirmations. Make a list of ten characteristics that you like about yourself and ten things that you do well.

| Characteristics that you like | Things that you do well |
|---|---|
| _____ | _____ |
| _____ | _____ |
| _____ | _____ |
| _____ | _____ |
| _____ | _____ |
| _____ | _____ |
| _____ | _____ |
| _____ | _____ |
| _____ | _____ |
| _____ | _____ |

In addition to reading your list of alternative or positive comments, read these self-affirming statements on a daily basis as well.

# Section XXV

# SINGLE PARENTS

Therapist's Overview

# SINGLE PARENTING—PRO OR CON?

## GOALS OF THE EXERCISE

1. Identify the pros and cons of being a single parent.
2. Reinforce within yourself that you can make it as a single parent.
3. Recognize what you can and cannot control and learn how to pick your battles.
4. Develop ways to nurture yourself on a regular basis.

## ADDITIONAL HOMEWORK THAT MAY BE APPLICABLE TO SINGLE PARENTS

- Anger Control Problems — Go Blow Out Some Candles — Page 31
- Caregiver Burnout — This Is for Me and That's Okay — Page 71
- Caregiver Burnout — What Drawer Does This Belong In? — Page 74

## ADDITIONAL PROBLEMS IN WHICH THIS EXERCISE MAY BE USEFUL

- Separation and Divorce

## SUGGESTIONS FOR PROCESSING THIS EXERCISE WITH THE CLIENT

Being a parent is the most difficult job in the world. Doing it alone is exponentially more difficult. Convey this important fact, but also highlight that surviving as a single parent is possible. To help him/her realize this, suggest the following exercise, which will help them in three specific ways (e.g., the goal referred to previously).

Exercise XXV.A

# SINGLE PARENTING—PRO OR CON?

As you already are too familiar with, being a parent is the most difficult job in the world. Doing it on your own can be doubly difficult (or easier, depending on what it was like before, when you had a spouse). Regardless, it is now just you and the kids. Surviving is a goal for most parents. It is possible, so don't give up hope. To make surviving more than just a hope and to make it a reality, you must be able to view it positively. The following exercise will help you evaluate the benefits and the limitations to being a single parent, as well as view being a single parent as a definite benefit.

1. Not having another adult to pitch in and help out with how to raise the kids can be an overwhelming reality. As with all things, however, there are pros and cons. Take a moment to recognize the pros and benefits and cons and limitations for you as a single parent today.

   | Pros | Cons |
   |------|------|
   |      |      |
   |      |      |
   |      |      |
   |      |      |
   |      |      |

2. Some of us can look at the same list, and what you have identified as a pro or benefit can be a con or limitation to someone else, the point being that perception plays a significant role in our thoughts, feelings, and reactions to our situations. One way to help with this is to pretend to be an attorney about to make a closing argument. As that attorney, your job is to describe your closing argument supporting the position of being a single parent. Review your list and record your argument.

   _____
   _____
   _____
   _____
   _____
   _____

**Therapist's Overview**

# WHAT DO I DO NOW?

## GOALS OF THE EXERCISE

1. Recognize what you can and cannot control and learn how to pick your battles.
2. Develop ways to nurture yourself on a regular basis.

## ADDITIONAL HOMEWORK THAT MAY BE APPLICABLE TO SINGLE PARENTS

- Anger Control Problems     Go Blow Out Some Candles     Page 31
- Caregiver Burnout     This Is for Me and That's Okay     Page 71
- Caregiver Burnout     What Drawer Does This Belong In?     Page 74

## ADDITIONAL PROBLEMS IN WHICH THIS EXERCISE MAY BE USEFUL

- Grief/Loss Unresolved
- Separation and Divorce

## SUGGESTIONS FOR PROCESSING THIS EXERCISE WITH THE CLIENT

Discuss with the group that as a single parent, there are obviously fewer shared responsibilities. Working, raising children, transporting children to their various activities, and trying to have a social life are just some of the responsibilities a single parent is expected to uphold. Explain to the group the importance of making time for themselves and learning what they have control over and how to deal with those things over which they do not have any control. The following exercise will help them get started.

**Exercise XXV.B**

# WHAT DO I DO NOW?

Being a single parent can be overwhelming at times when you think about all of the responsibilities and expectations you carry around. That is why it is important to develop a sense of what you have control over and what you do not. This can significantly lighten your load. Once you are aware of what you really can control you need to be able to prioritize. Part of being able to successfully prioritize involves good time management skills. The following exercise will help you in getting started on these tasks as well as help you to include ways for you to take care of you.

1. What can you control? Some might say nothing. Others will attempt to control everything. As in most cases, choosing a middle ground is generally a better choice. Therefore, your first step is to start accepting that there are some things you can and some things that you cannot control in your life. Over the next two or three days keep a diary of what you do and what happens in your life. For example:

   *My daughter decided not to take a nap today and the two hours I had planned to do work did not happen. I then went to a meeting, which went well. An afternoon client canceled so I got to go to the gym. Just in this short excerpt, the only thing I had control over doing was going to the gym. I could not force my daughter to take a nap and I could not make my client keep an appointment.*

   Record your experiences in a notebook or diary. After each entry, decide which things you had control over and which things you did not.

2. Approximately how much time did you feel frustrated or angry or upset about the things that you could not control?

   _____

3. What could you have been doing during the time that you were feeling upset, angry, or frustrated?

   _____
   _____

4. This is just a small example to demonstrate that sometimes we utilize our time inefficiently and unproductively. The more aware you become of what you can and cannot control in your life, the more productive you will be with your time.

Exercise XXV.B

5. Write down the things that are important to you (e.g., spending time with my children, working, reading a book or magazine, going to the gym, talking to friends or neighbors, etc.).

   _____
   _____
   _____
   _____
   _____
   _____
   _____

6. Prioritize your list.

   _____
   _____
   _____
   _____
   _____
   _____
   _____
   _____

7. How much time do you spend and how much time do you want to spend doing each of the activities that you listed?

   | Activity/expectation | Time I do spend | Time I want to spend |
   |---|---|---|
   | _____ | _____ | _____ |
   | _____ | _____ | _____ |
   | _____ | _____ | _____ |
   | _____ | _____ | _____ |
   | _____ | _____ | _____ |
   | _____ | _____ | _____ |
   | _____ | _____ | _____ |
   | _____ | _____ | _____ |

Exercise XXV.B

8. Over the next week, make a plan that complies with the activities you have listed and the time that you want to spend doing them or what you want to do to meet that expectation. For example:

   | Activity/expectation | Time or activity |
   |---|---|
   | Play with the children more. | Tuesday night we will play a board game together before bed. |

   Remember to focus on what you can control.

9. Often, as parents we overlook our own needs or rarely get around to meeting our needs. When this happens we add to our own stress level. When we are stressed, we tend to have a more difficult time with our daily life. It is extremely important to remember *you* and how to nurture yourself. To help with this process, use the following space to identify those things that make you feel good (e.g., taking a bubble bath, going to dinner, talking with a friend, etc.).

   _____
   _____
   _____
   _____
   _____

10. Over the next week, schedule times when you will engage in at least three of the above self-nurturing activities.

11. Over the next week, schedule times when you will engage in at least three of the above self-nurturing activities.

    | Activity | Day That I Will Do This Activity |
    |---|---|
    |  |  |
    |  |  |
    |  |  |

# Section XXVI

# TOXIC PARENT SURVIVORS

Therapist's Overview

# I AM GETTING RID OF THESE OLD TAPES—PART ONE

## GOALS OF THE EXERCISE

1. Identify the negative thoughts and feelings associated with the comments and names your abusive parent or guardian would tell you while growing up.
2. Identify how you would describe yourself as a child.
3. Identify the positive qualities that you and others see in you as an adult.
4. Become aware of the times that you view yourself as how your abusive parent or guardian would describe you.
5. Learn ways to redirect and replace such negative depictions of yourself with positive comebacks and self-affirming cognitions.

## ADDITIONAL HOMEWORK THAT MAY BE APPLICABLE TO TOXIC PARENT SURVIVORS

- Adult Children of Alcoholics    What's My Role?         Page 3
- Incest Survivors—Adult           What I Need to Tell You  Page 179

## ADDITIONAL PROBLEMS IN WHICH THIS EXERCISE MAY BE USEFUL

- Domestic Violence Survivors
- Incest Survivors—Adult

## SUGGESTIONS FOR PROCESSING THIS EXERCISE WITH THE CLIENT

The negative comments our parents made to us growing up can be like never-ending audiotapes that never turn off in our heads. After enough time, we tend to start believing such comments as reality. The following exercise is geared to help group members to identify these old tapes and learn ways of replacing them with new and more affirming tapes.

**Exercise XXVI.A**

# I AM GETTING RID OF THESE OLD TAPES—PART ONE

The negative comments our parents made to us growing up can be like never-ending audiotapes that never turn off in our heads. After enough time, we tend to start believing such comments as reality. The following exercise is geared to help you get rid of those old tapes and learn ways to replace them with new and more self-affirming tapes.

1. Describe the earliest recollection of something your abusive parent said to you and that still resounds in your head today. Describe how old you were and the context within which the negative comment(s) was made.

   _____
   _____
   _____
   _____

2. In looking back at this time, describe how you as an adult would describe you as that child. For example, your abusive parent may have said something like, "You stupid kid, why are you always getting into my tool box and messing things up? You couldn't fix anything anyway." You as an adult today might look back on this and think, "I was just a 6-year-old kid trying to take my training wheels off. I was thinking how proud my parents would be of me if I could do it all on my own."

   _____
   _____
   _____
   _____

3. Describe three or four other times in which your abusive parent or guardian said or did something negative to you and that still stands out in your mind today.

   _____
   _____
   _____
   _____
   _____
   _____

Exercise XXVI.A

4. Repeat step 2 for each situation you just described in item 3.

5. For each negative situation you described, replace your abusive parent or guardian with a loving and nurturing adult figure. Rewrite what your abusive parent or guardian said or did with a more positive and caring response that a loving and nurturing adult would have said or done. For example, "Hey, sweetheart, you are trying so hard to get those training wheels off, would you like me to help you?"

6. Review these newly revised versions of those memories on a daily basis as a way to create "new tapes" to play in your head.

7. Over the next week, keep track of the times you begin to view yourself as your abusive parent or guardian would. For example, "When I forgot to pack my daughter's lunch today I called myself a stupid idiot, just like my abusive parent or guardian would have described me."

8. For each negative depiction of yourself that you have described, write a more understanding and realistic depiction of yourself on the following lines. For example, "I was so hurried today that I totally forgot to pack my daughter's lunch. I'll make sure that I remember tomorrow."

9. Thinking of yourself now as an adult, what are the positive qualities and characteristics you have and/or that others have described you as having?

10. Read this list two to three times a day as another way to create new tapes.

Therapist's Overview

# I AM GETTING RID OF THESE OLD TAPES—PART TWO

## GOALS OF THE EXERCISE

1. Identify the thoughts and feelings you have toward the parent who did not protect you from your abusive parent.
2. Be able to express those thoughts and feelings in letter form. (Deciding to mail it should be discussed as a therapeutic intervention. This may not be in the best interest of the client.)

## ADDITIONAL HOMEWORK THAT MAY BE APPLICABLE TO TOXIC PARENT SURVIVORS

- Adult Children of Alcoholics   What's My Role?            Page 3
- Incest Survivors—Adult         What I Need to Tell You    Page 179

## ADDITIONAL PROBLEMS IN WHICH THIS EXERCISE MAY BE USEFUL

- Incest Survivors—Adult

## SUGGESTIONS FOR PROCESSING THIS EXERCISE WITH THE CLIENT

Clients also need to be able to identify and give voice to the thoughts and feelings they have regarding the parent who did not protect them growing up from the abusive parent. Some clients may have already dealt with this and describe their relationship with their nonabusive parent as fair or even good. This assignment may be used to review how they achieved that forgiveness. For those who are still troubled by the lack of action taken by the nonabusive parent, suggest completing this exercise as a way to bring some closure to this issue.

Exercise XXVI.B

# I AM GETTING RID OF THESE OLD TAPES—PART TWO

Sometimes when one parent is abusive, the other parent is nurturing and caring. However, that caring parent sometimes is unable, for whatever reasons, to intervene and stop the abuse from continuing. You may have questioned why this was the case. A variety of feelings often develop toward this nonabusive parent. As a way of healing and possibly strengthening your relationship with your nonabusive parent, complete the following exercise. It is designed to help you identify and give voice to the thoughts and feelings you have carried with you over the years.

1. In thinking back to the earliest recollection you have of something your abusive parent said to you or did to you, describe what your other parent was doing.

   _____
   _____
   _____
   _____

2. What feelings do you experience now regarding your nonabusive parent while remembering this event?

   _____
   _____
   _____

3. If you could rewrite that memory, what would you have had your nonabusive parent do and/or say?

   _____
   _____
   _____

Exercise XXVI.B

4. Think about three or four other times in which your abusive parent or guardian said or did something negative to you and describe what your other parent was doing or saying. If your other parent was not present, describe what he/she did when he/she found out what happened.

   _____
   _____
   _____
   _____
   _____
   _____
   _____

5. Repeat step 3 and rewrite each troubling memory so that you can create a new and more nurturing ending for each memory you identified in item 3.

   _____
   _____
   _____
   _____
   _____
   _____
   _____
   _____
   _____
   _____

6. In thinking about these memories, what thoughts are going through your mind? Write these down.

   _____
   _____
   _____
   _____

7. What feelings are you experiencing? List them.

   _____
   _____
   _____
   _____
   _____

Exercise XXVI.B

8. Put your thoughts and feelings together and describe what you would like to say to the parent who did not protect you the way you deserved and needed.

9. In thinking about these memories, describe what you would want to say to the parent who was abusive.

# Section XXVII

# TYPE-A STRESS

Therapist's Overview

# WHERE'S MY TENSION?

## GOALS OF THE EXERCISE

1. Recognize that stress can result from changes in your environment and your bodies, as well as your thoughts.
2. Identify how stress can be found in your environment, body, and thoughts.
3. Track daily stressors as a way of increasing your awareness of such stress factors.

## ADDITIONAL HOMEWORK THAT MAY BE APPLICABLE TO TYPE-A STRESS

- Anger Control Problems    Go Blow Out Some Candles                 Page 31
- Assertiveness Deficit     Is It Passive, Aggressive, or Assertive? Page 46

## ADDITIONAL PROBLEMS IN WHICH THIS EXERCISE MAY BE USEFUL

- Anger Control Problems
- Anxiety
- Parenting Problems

## SUGGESTIONS FOR PROCESSING THIS EXERCISE WITH THE CLIENT

Explain to group members that stress can be brought on by many factors. The primary factors involve one's environment, body, and thoughts. To reduce one's stress, he/she must first become aware of when and in what form it is occurring. The following exercise is designed to help individuals increase their awareness of their stress and its origins.

Exercise XXVII.A

# WHERE'S MY TENSION?

This exercise is designed to help you identify when you are feeling stressed, as well as the origin of that stress. You will need a journal to complete this exercise.

**Where is the tension in my body?**

1. Rate the level of stress you are feeling right now on a scale of 0 to 10. Let a rating of zero (0) represent no stress whatsoever. Let a rating of 10 represent stress that is so overwhelming that you feel as if you will explode any moment.

    My current stress level rate is a _____.

2. Scan your body by closing your eyes and visualizing each part from your toes up to your head (e.g., toes and feet, shins and calves, thighs, stomach, chest, arms, neck, head). Identify which areas feel tense or tight.

    The following body areas feel tense or tight: _____.

    How else might you describe the tension in your body?
    _____

**What areas in my life create tension for me?**

3. Over the next three or four days, keep track of your daily activities and rate how stressful each activity is. Include driving to work, making phone calls, meetings, paperwork, lunch dates, dinner with others, exercise, and so forth—anything that you do over the next three or four days.

| Activity | Stress-level rating |
|---|---|
| _____ | _____ |
| _____ | _____ |
| _____ | _____ |
| _____ | _____ |
| _____ | _____ |

Exercise XXVII.A

**What goes through my mind when I am feeling stressed?**

4. Over the next two or three days, keep track of anything that you would rate between 5 and 10 on your level-of-stress scale. You can also review the stressful activities you listed in item 3. For any of these that you rated 5 or higher, describe what was going through your mind.

| Activity | Thoughts |
|----------|----------|
|          |          |
|          |          |
|          |          |
|          |          |
|          |          |
|          |          |

**Therapist's Overview**

# WHEN I FEEL TENSION/STRESS I CAN...

## GOALS OF THE EXERCISE

1. Decrease the tension in your body.
2. Feel more relaxed.
3. Identify ways to redirect thoughts that maintain and/or escalate the tension and stress.

## ADDITIONAL HOMEWORK THAT MAY BE APPLICABLE TO TYPE-A STRESS

- Anger Control Problems    Go Blow Out Some Candles    Page 31
- Assertiveness Deficit    Is It Passive, Aggressive, or Assertive?    Page 46

## ADDITIONAL PROBLEMS IN WHICH THIS EXERCISE MAY BE USEFUL

- Anger Control Problems
- Anxiety
- Parenting Problems

## SUGGESTIONS FOR PROCESSING THIS EXERCISE WITH THE CLIENT

Once a person identifies how their body reacts under stress, they need to know how to reduce such stress and tension. Describe the idea of progressive muscle relaxation. The following exercise can be used to help individuals learn how to relax each muscle group and continue to do so in between sessions. You will also need to review with group members what are cognitive distortions or thinking errors and how these contribute to stress. Before suggesting this assignment to any individual, make sure that their physical condition does not limit them in any way. Ask each member if they can tense their body and relax it without feeling pain. If any individual reports feeling pain, recommend that they consult their physician.

Exercise XXVII.B

# WHEN I FEEL TENSION/STRESS I CAN . . .

Most people can indicate a part of their body that absorbs the tension whenever they are feeling stressed. In addition, most of us can identify the various thoughts that run through our minds when we are stressed. These thoughts can sometimes maintain and escalate your feelings of tension and stress. The following exercise will help you to release that tension and any other tension in your body, as well as learn ways to redirect those thoughts that can contribute to maintaining and increasing your tension and stress.*

## HOW TO REDUCE THE TENSION IN YOUR BODY

Frequently, our bodies react to stress before we even realize that we are stressed. By practicing the following exercise, you will learn to become more aware of when your body is getting tighter or tense and how to relax. The idea of this exercise is to first learn how your body feels when you are tense as well as when you are relaxed. The more you practice experiencing both states (relaxed and tense), the more control you will have over which state you want to be in.

1. With both hands make a fist and squeeze as tight as you can. Hold that tension and count to 20. When you get to 20, release your grip and point your fingers down to the ground. Do this one more time.
2. Describe what you felt when you were making a fist and what you felt when you released your fists.

_____

_____

The feeling that you just experienced was that of tension and relaxation. These are two opposites and cannot occur simultaneously. When any part of your body is tense, you can learn how to relax it. The sooner you become aware of your body becoming tense, the sooner and easier you will be able to relax. To learn this you must practice tensing and relaxing each part of your body. The following exercise will walk you through each body part.

3. Start with your feet. Have a seat and imagine your feet gripping the floor or picking up a pencil with your toes. Hold that tenseness for 10 seconds and then release it.

---

*If you have any physical problems, you should get clearance from your personal physician on whether you can do the following exercise. If at any time you feel uncomfortable, discontinue this exercise.*

4. Move up to your shins and calves. While sitting in the chair, lift your legs about 6 to 12 inches off the floor. Point your toes up and back toward your knees as if you were going to have your toes touch your knees. You can also push your feet down as if you were making a straight line from your hips down to your toes. Hold for 10 seconds and then release.
5. Move up to your thighs. While sitting upright and with your back straight, lift your legs as high as you can. Feel your thighs getting tighter and tighter. Hold it for 10 seconds and then release.
6. Move up to your abdomen. Imagine doing a situp or a crunch, and squeeze your abdomen as tightly as you can. Hold this for 10 seconds and then release.
7. Move up to your chest. Imagine that you are squeezing a big rubber ball in front of your chest. As you are squeezing the imaginary ball, also imagine squeezing and tightening your chest. Hold this for 10 seconds and then release.
8. Move up to your shoulders. Raise your shoulder as if you want to touch your ears. You should feel tension in your shoulders as well as part of your neck. Hold it for 10 seconds and then release.
9. Move to your arms. Make a fist, turn your fists toward you so that the back of your hands are facing away from you. Curl your fists toward your shoulders. You should feel tension in your biceps and forearms. Hold this for 10 seconds and then release. Make a fist again. This time, hold your arms by your side and straighten your arms so that you feel tension in your triceps. Hold this for 10 seconds and then release.
10. Move to your face. Close your eyes tightly together. Hold for 10 seconds and then release.
11. You have now moved from your toes to your head and tensed each body part and relaxed it. Practice this at least once a day.

## HOW TO REDUCE AND REDIRECT THE THOUGHTS WHICH MAINTAIN AND POSSIBLY INCREASE MY STRESS AND TENSION

12. If you have not done so, over the next three days, track the thoughts that go through your mind whenever you are feeling stressed. Record what those thoughts were.

    When I feel stressed, these are the thoughts that go through my mind:

    _____
    _____
    _____
    _____
    _____
    _____
    _____

13. For each thought that you listed, write a disputing comment. For example, if your stressful thought is, "I can't believe this is happening to me, nothing ever goes the way

Exercise XXVII.B

I plan it," your disputing comment might be, "This really sucks and I can't stand it when things go wrong. I will need to do my best and just get through it. I have done it before, I can do it again." The disputing comments are to be positive and encouraging.

_____
_____
_____
_____
_____
_____
_____

14. You may also need to practice ways to stop thinking negative when you are feeling stressed. A couple ways that you can do this include:
    - Snap a rubber band around your wrist each time that you think a negative thought.
    - Shout *stop,* either in your head or out loud.
15. Review with your group and therapist other thought-stopping techniques.
16. Put the thought-stopping techniques and the disputing comments together as a way to stop and redirect negative thinking.

# Section XXVIII

# VOCATIONAL STRESS

Therapist's Overview

# WHAT ELSE CAN I DO TO MAKE THINGS BETTER?

## GOALS OF THE EXERCISE

1. Identify the pattern of conflict at work.
2. Identify the possible responses to deal with the conflict.
3. Identify those responses that are most likely to improve the situation at work.

## ADDITIONAL HOMEWORK THAT MAY BE APPLICABLE TO VOCATIONAL STRESS

- Anger Control Problems    Is It Anger or Aggression?    Page 27
- Phobias—Specific/Social   Let's Float with It           Page 212
- Type-A Stress             Where's My Tension?           Page 263

## ADDITIONAL PROBLEMS IN WHICH THIS EXERCISE MAY BE USEFUL

- Separation and Divorce

## SUGGESTIONS FOR PROCESSING THIS EXERCISE WITH CLIENT

The following exercise is designed to help group members identify the pattern of interaction that takes place at work when there is conflict. Once they have identified this, they are to develop possible alternative responses that may improve their situation. Group members should be encouraged to identify these alternatives with other peers, family members, and other support persons.

# Exercise XXVIII.A

# WHAT ELSE CAN I DO TO MAKE THINGS BETTER?

The following exercise is to assist you in identifying the pattern of negative interaction that takes place at work when there is a conflict. This conflict might be between you and other coworkers, subordinates, supervisors, or customers. The exercise is based on a general problem-solving approach. You will first be asked to identify the problem and also to describe your response and those involved. You will then be asked to describe other options regarding how you could respond. The next step is to pick one of the options you believe will improve the situation and test it out.

## STEP 1: DESCRIBE THE PROBLEM

1. Describe the conflict(s) you have at work.

    Whom do they involve?
    _____

    When do they tend to occur (morning, during certain meetings, etc.)?
    _____
    _____

2. Describe a recent conflict. Who was involved and what did he/she do?
    _____
    _____
    _____
    _____
    _____
    _____
    _____

    What did you say or do?
    _____
    _____
    _____

How did the other person involved respond to what you said and/or did?

How did the situation end?

How did you feel about this interaction?

How do you think the other person felt?

## STEP 2: LIST ALTERNATIVES

3. Try to describe at least three other responses or reactions that you could have engaged in, which would have reduced the conflict (e.g., using "I" statements, apologizing for your part in the conflict, etc.). You may want to ask other peers, family members, or others with whom you feel comfortable for additional ideas.

## STEP 3: PICK ONE OF THE ALTERNATIVES

4. Which of these alternatives will you pick to try during the next conflict?

## STEP 4: TRY THE ALTERNATIVE

5. Practice this option with a friend or family member to learn how the other person might respond to you.
6. Use this alternative the next time you encounter a conflict.

Exercise XXVIII.A

## STEP 5: EVALUATE THE EFFECTIVENESS OF THE ALTERNATIVE

7. After you have tried this different approach, evaluate its effectiveness. Describe what was good, as well as what was not so good.

   _____
   _____
   _____
   _____
   _____

8. You should also try one or two other alternatives and determine which ones work best for you. The more alternatives you have to choose from, the less stressed you will be.

Therapist's Overview

# HOW I WILL GET WHAT I WANT

## GOALS OF THE EXERCISE

1. Identify your skills and personal qualities.
2. Identify your interests within the workforce.
3. Identify the barriers to succeeding in your employment situation.
4. Increase your sense of self-esteem and hope regarding your employment situation.

## ADDITIONAL HOMEWORK THAT MAY BE APPLICABLE TO VOCATIONAL STRESS

- Anger Control Problems        Is It Anger or Aggression?      Page 27
- Phobias—Specific/Social       Let's Float with It             Page 212
- Type-A Stress                 Where's My Tension?             Page 263

## ADDITIONAL PROBLEMS IN WHICH THIS EXERCISE MAY BE USEFUL

- Separation and Divorce (individuals trying to start over in the job market)

## SUGGESTIONS FOR PROCESSING THIS EXERCISE WITH THE CLIENT

This exercise is designed to give individuals a way of developing a plan to succeed by identifying the skills needed, as well as the barriers to progressing. It is very rational and follows a problem-solving approach.

Exercise XXVIII.B

# HOW I WILL GET WHAT I WANT

Most of us continually strive to get ahead. To do this, it is sometimes beneficial to devise a plan. To help you in developing this plan, the following exercise will guide you in answering various questions. When you have answered all the questions, you will be able to develop the plan you need to succeed.

1. To identify what your work style is, ask yourself some of the following questions:

    How do I like to work? (Fast-paced? Slow-paced?)

    What type of environment do I work best in? (Team environment? Individual?)

    What type of management do I prefer? (Hands on? Hands off?)

    How do I like to communicate? (Present to large groups? Present to small groups? Prefer no formal presentations at all? Prefer communication in writing?)

    Describe your work style based on the information and answers to the preceding questions.

    _____
    _____
    _____
    _____

2. To identify what motivates you, ask yourself some of the following questions:

    What makes me get out of bed in the morning?

    Am I working for a promotion, award, or a pat on the back?

    Am I satisfied with meeting job expectations, or do I want to consistently exceed them?

    Describe on the following lines what motivates you.

    _____
    _____
    _____
    _____
    _____

Exercise XXVIII.B

3. To identify what skills you have, ask yourself some of the following questions:

   What am I good at? (Computers? Writing?)

   Which skills that I have do I want to use on the job?

   Describe your skills.

   _____
   _____
   _____
   _____
   _____

4. To identify what internal barriers and/or developmental needs you have, ask yourself some of the following questions:

   What is stopping me from getting where I want to go at work?

   Do I have preconceived notions about individuals who are needed in certain departments (i.e., no one from this department has ever gotten into that department; or I don't have that set of skills, so they won't want me in that department)?

   What do I need to develop or learn to get where I want to go?

   How much am I willing to do to get what I want at work?

   Describe the internal barriers and/or needs that you have in order to progress at work.

   _____
   _____
   _____
   _____
   _____

Once you have been able to assess your style, motivation, skills, internal barriers, and developmental needs, you can begin to develop a plan to move forward in your career. You will be better able to look at jobs current or future and determine whether they are a fit or if there are things you can do to make it a fit.

# ABOUT THE AUTHOR

**Louis J. Bevilacqua, Psy.D., NCC,** is the Clinical Director of Connections Adolescent and Family Care, a private psychotherapy practice in Exton, Pennsylvania. He specializes in the treatment of families and couples, as well as behavioral disordered youth, depression, cutting, and suicide. His previous publications include *Comparative Treatments for Relationship Dysfunction* (Springer, 2000), and *The Brief Family Therapy Homework Planner* (John Wiley & Sons, 2001), both of which were coedited with Frank Dattilio, Ph.D.

# ABOUT THE DOWNLOADABLE ASSIGNMENTS

Thank you for choosing the Wiley Practice*Planners*® series. *Group Therapy Homework Planner's* website includes all the book's exercises in Word format for your convenience. To access the assignments, please follow these steps:

**Step 1** Go to www.wiley.com/go/hwpassignments
**Step 2** Enter your email address, the password provided below, and click "submit"
Password: group2015
**Step 3** Select and download the listed exercises

If you need any assistance, please contact Wiley Customer Care 800-762-2974 (U.S.), 317-572-3994 (International) or visit www.wiley.com.